Simply Sarasota

CREATIVELY CASUAL CUISINE

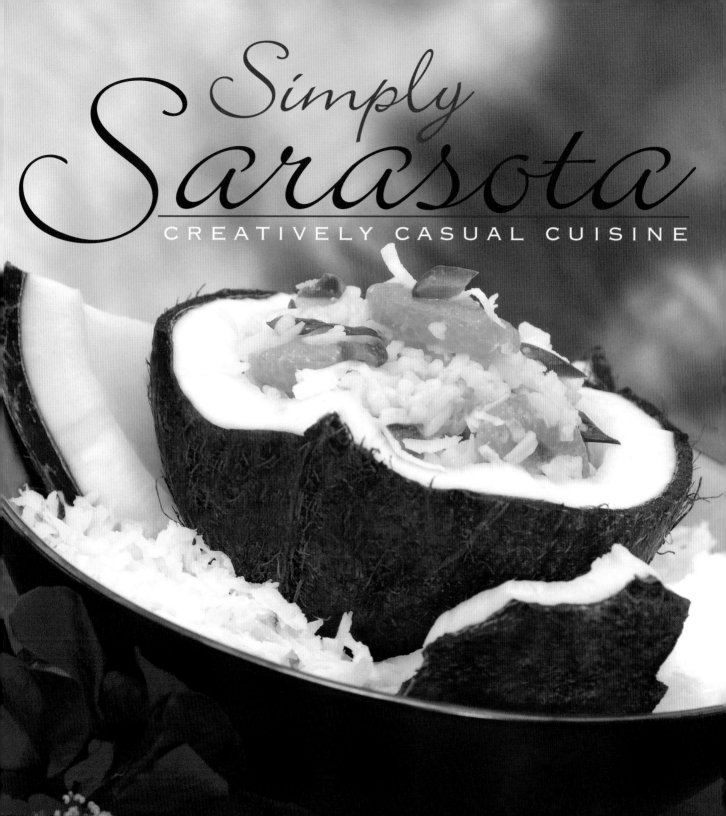

Simply Sarasota

CREATIVELY CASUAL CUISINE

JUNIOR LEAGUE OF SARASOTA

Simply Sarasota
CREATIVELY CASUAL CUISINE

Published by Junior League of Sarasota
Copyright © 2007 by Junior League of Sarasota
3300 South Tamiami Trail, Suite 3
Sarasota, Florida 34239
941-953-5600

PHOTOGRAPHY © BY BARBARA BANKS PHOTOGRAPHY
(Photographs on pages 66 and 67 used by permission of the John & Mable Ringling Museum)
PHOTOGRAPHY ASSISTANT: KATHRYN BRASS
FOOD STYLIST: JENNIFER AHEARN-KOCH
COPY EDITOR: DIANE MUHLFELD

The Junior League of Sarasota, Inc., is an organization of women committed to promoting voluntarism, developing the potential of women, and improving the community through the effective action and leadership of trained volunteers. Its purpose is exclusively educational and charitable.

The Junior League of Sarasota reaches out to women of all races, religions, and national origins who demonstrate an interest in and commitment to voluntarism.

Each recipe has been tested for accuracy and excellence. We do not claim that all of the recipes are original, only that they are our favorites. We regret that we were unable to include many recipes submitted, due to similarity or lack of space.

For those readers looking for healthier choices, nutritional profiles have been provided for some of our recipes and can be found on those recipe pages.

Library of Congress Control Number: 2006925549
ISBN-10: 0-9779104-0-7
ISBN-13: 978-0-9779104-0-3

Edited, Designed, and Manufactured by
Favorite Recipes® Press
An imprint of

FRP

P.O. Box 305142
Nashville, Tennessee 37230
800-358-0560

ART DIRECTOR: STEVE NEWMAN
BOOK DESIGN: SHERI FERGUSON
PROJECT EDITOR: LINDA BENNIE

Manufactured in China   First Printing 2007   10,000 copies

Simply Sarasota
CREATIVELY CASUAL CUISINE

EXECUTIVE CHEF SPONSORS

MAÎTRE D' SPONSORS

CHEF DE CUISINE SPONSORS

Michael & Stacey Corley

PASTRY CHEF SPONSORS

| First Watch Restaurants | Michael's On East | Simply Sarasota Cookbook Committee | Sunset Automotive Group |

SAUTÉ CHEF SPONSORS

Al Purmort Insurance, Inc.	Tanya Marks Foster	Tom & Debbie Shapiro
Cheryl Burstein	Junior Welfare League of Sarasota	Olivia Thomas & Patrick Frye
Andy & Valerie Dorr	Junior League of Sarasota Sustaining Council	Jim & Jennifer Vett
Bonnie Early	Connie S. Parker	Louis & Elizabeth Wery
	Elaine M. Rice	

SALAD CHEF SPONSORS

Donna M. Baranowski	Century Bank	Horizon Title Services	Dr. Patricia Sabers
Fran & Jamie Becker	Beth Cannata & Amie Shay	Cindy Kaiser	Sandi Stewart
Bruce & Lisa Beckstein	James & Kim Cornetet	Mary Ann Lockhart	Amanda E. Stiff
Debbi Benedict	Connie Cosbar	Melinda "Mindy" Mast	Jo Strobel
Barbara W. Billings	The Ecology Group, Inc.	Caryn Patterson	Dorothy B. Stuart
Anne Braman	Susan Featherman	Shirley A. Ritchey	Norma G. Wemmer
Lee Byron	Christie Giuffra	Martha B. Rogers	
	Marcia Goldstein	Teresa Z. Saba	

CHEF APPRENTICE SPONSORS

| Mary-Lou Moulton | Sharon Rolle | Lisa Ward | Elizabeth Wildhack |

Special Thanks

The *Simply Sarasota* Committee would like to extend its sincere appreciation to everyone who supported the creation of this very special book. We are so fortunate to have had the loving support of our spouses, families, friends, and neighbors throughout this process and are equally indebted to our fellow Junior League members who offered their assistance at every turn. The Committee offers a heartfelt thank-you to the Junior League members and friends who so graciously opened up their kitchens by sharing and testing their favorite recipes. We are especially grateful to the generous sponsors who gave their overwhelming financial and moral support.

Simply Sarasota is truly a collaborative effort that represents the best of Sarasota and the generosity of its people. Thank you to all of its contributors, great and small.

Acknowledgments

PHOTOGRAPHY:	Barbara Banks
PHOTOGRAPHY ASSISTANT:	Kathryn Brass
FOOD STYLIST:	Jennifer Ahearn-Koch
FOOD PHOTOGRAPHY PREPARATION:	Chef Douglas C. Ricciardi
FOOD PHOTOGRAPHY LOCATION:	Mattison's Steakhouse at the Plaza
COPY EDITOR:	Diane Muhlfeld
ACCESSORIES:	Linens-N-Things

Previous Cookbook by the Junior League of Sarasota: *Fare by the Sea*, First Printing 1983

Special thanks to the following contributing chefs, wine experts, restaurants, and writers:

Chef Joseph Askew—recipe
Chef Jean-Jacques Barilleau—recipe
Amy A. Elder—non-recipe text
First Watch Restaurant—recipe
Chef Ralph Flores—recipe, tips
Marsha Fottler—non-recipe text
Beth Fox—coffee tips
Fred's—recipe
Judi Gallagher—tips
Kevin Hall—recipe
Michael Klauber—recipe, wine tips
Latitude 23.5 Fine Coffee & Tea—recipe
Kelly Liebel—non-recipe text
Lori Manning—graphic art

Chef Mario Martinez—recipe
Chef Paul Mattison—recipes, tips
Mattison's™—recipe
Michael's On East—recipes
Liza Morrow— non-recipe text
Chef Laurent Moussa—recipes
Kristine Nickel—foreword, wine tips
Northern Trust Bank—recipe
Chef James Plocharsky—recipe
Sandi Stewart— non-recipe text
Stonewood Grill & Tavern—recipe
Troyer's Dutch Heritage—recipe
Chef Jay Weinstein—wine pairings

Cookbook Committee

CO-CHAIR
Stacey Corley

CO-CHAIR
Tanya Marks Foster

RECIPE TEXT
Sharon Ehrlich, chair
Nancy Bailey
Jenny Hime
Cynthia Miner
Sarah Paul
Cerita Purmort
Gretchen Reimel-Moussa
Dee Dee Rice
Debbie Shapiro
Sheryl Vieira

NON-RECIPE TEXT
Ellie Rochford, chair
Genevieve Hall
Allison Stewart

PHOTOGRAPHY/ART
Chellie Barilleau
Patty Sabers
Evan Schulte

SPECIAL EVENTS/PROMOTIONS
Cheryl Burstein
Kristy Duvall

SECRETARY/COMMUNICATIONS
Dee Dee Rice

TREASURER/FINANCE
Lydia Chapdelain

SUSTAINER LIAISON
Cerita Purmort

JLS FINANCE VICE-PRESIDENT 2004–2006
Jennifer Vett

JLS PRESIDENT 2004–2005
Dee Dee Rice

JLS PRESIDENT 2005–2006
Valerie Dorr

JLS PRESIDENT 2006–2007
Olivia Thomas

JUNIOR LEAGUE OF SARASOTA
Women building better communities

Foreword

I was recently coerced into "cleaning out" my cookbooks. Their numbers had grown well into the triple digits, and with an equal number of wine books, the sheer volume was threatening to take over the kitchen. This, of course, was not my idea, but I obliged grudgingly and soon found myself cross-legged on my kitchen floor, surrounded by piles of cookbooks of every shape and size.

It turned out to be a glorious afternoon. Like photographs, most every cookbook had its own story that brought back such wonderful memories. I quickly realized that the best were those collected during travels across the United States, trips when a stop in a quaint bookstore would yield a cookbook that highlighted the particular city or region—its local customs, local foodstuffs, and local attitudes about cooking. Invariably, many of those cookbooks were published by the local Junior League.

Junior League cookbooks do capture the local essence because they are written by local cooks. It does not matter if you are a long- or short-time resident or just traveling through; the cookbook becomes a snapshot of the region and an interactive partner in creating memories, not just of that moment, but in the present and future, as well. Could you ask for a more collaborative companion?

During my massive sorting out, I pounced upon *Tell Me More*, published by the Junior League of Lafayette, Louisiana. Not only did I have the pleasure of picturing a wonderful bookstore in New Iberia where the cookbook was purchased, but I recalled also a Cajun dinner party I gave, with the menu borrowed from the pages of *Tell Me More*. The aromas of Cajun Crawfish Cornbread practically wafted off the page, and I longed for the taste of the Chicken and Sausage Jambalaya I'd prepared. I even thought of those Cajun martinis, and their aftermath.

Sarasota is now poised to reassert its culinary prowess with *Simply Sarasota: Creatively Casual Cuisine*, the first Junior League cookbook from our chapter since 1983. League members eagerly took on the mantle of "foodie" as they scoured their recipe cards in search of the perfect offerings for this very special volume. The mission was tough, yet achievable: recipes that portray what is so special about Sarasota, the physical beauty that draws us to this beautiful place, and the cultural *carte du jour* that keeps us so stimulated. Inside these pages you will find recipes that showcase our elegant-yet-casual cuisine in the settings that inspire our passion for this slice of the Gulf Coast. You will become acquainted with some of our treasures—the John and Mable Ringling Museum of Art, Selby Gardens, and our fabulous beaches to name a few. And, the foods these resources call to mind will engage your senses. Read on, and prepare to make memories, too.

Kristine

Kristine Nickel has been writing about food and wine since 1983, when she began writing the Grapevine, *the Chicago Tribune's weekly wine column. In 1990, Nickel moved to Sarasota, where she had vacationed since 1969. She quickly took up a culinary role as a dining-out critic and is currently a local food and wine editor.*

Introduction

Simply Sarasota: Creatively Casual Cuisine is a unique cookbook reflecting the essence of Sarasota—an elegant, but casual city abundant in natural beauty. Visitors are irresistibly drawn to its world-famous white sandy beaches, its broad range and number of cultural offerings, and the rich diversity of its residents. Through this cookbook, you'll experience Sarasota's culinary heritage first-hand while supporting the mission of the Junior League of Sarasota (JLS). This mission, like that of other Junior Leagues around the world, is to promote voluntarism, develop the potential of women, and improve the community through the effective action and leadership of trained volunteers.

The JLS, formerly known as the Junior Welfare League, was formed in Sarasota in 1957 by a small group of dedicated women seeking to improve their community. Nineteen years later it was admitted into what is now known as the Association of Junior Leagues International (AJLI). Over the ensuing decades, JLS membership and participation continued to grow and thrive. League members have created a legacy as visionary problem-solvers by developing projects that have become formidable institutions in Sarasota. The organization has contributed energetically to a wide range of civic and human service initiatives, as well as a host of projects and programs in collaboration with other community partners and agencies. A snapshot of past projects includes the following:

- Developing the Sarasota Day Nursery (now known as Children First) to provide quality child-care for at-risk children
- Establishing the traveling historical museum that became the nucleus for the permanent museum at Historic Spanish Point
- Creating the Partnerships and Alliances Linking Schools (PALS) program, which provides schools with trained volunteer resources to aid classroom teachers
- Creating Teen Court, which addresses juvenile crime issues at the peer level in a professional county courtroom setting
- Improving local parks and providing safe places for children to play, including developing the first handicapped-accessible playground
- Restoring residential units at a transitional housing complex for adults returning to independent living
- Developing a school literacy project, tailored to individual schools, with the goal of improving student achievement, recognized with one of two Community Impact Awards presented by AJLI in 2005

The enthusiastic members of the JLS volunteer thousands of hours each year and have raised more than $1 million to support community projects. Proceeds from the sales of *Simply Sarasota: Creatively Casual Cuisine* will help the JLS maintain its steadfast dedication to enriching Sarasota's wonderful community. Your purchase has helped the League promote its vision and mission. The members of the JLS wish you many enjoyable hours savoring the essence of Sarasota. *Bon appétit!*

Contents

Crab-Stuffed Endive, page 15

Simply Starters

DILLED SHRIMP

1 large red onion, thinly sliced
1 1/4 cups mayonnaise
1/2 cup sour cream
1/3 cup lemon juice
1/4 cup sugar

2 tablespoons dried dill weed
1/4 teaspoon salt
2 pounds cooked shrimp, peeled
  and deveined

Combine the onion, mayonnaise, sour cream, lemon juice, sugar, dill weed and salt in a large bowl and mix well. Fold in the shrimp and chill, covered, for 8 to 10 hours. Stir once and serve with wooden picks.

Note: To make this recipe lighter, use light mayonnaise, a sugar substitute, and reduced-fat sour cream. Fresh dill weed and lemon juice will enhance the flavors, and the fat won't be missed at all.

Yield: 8 to 10 servings

MINIATURE PASTRY SHELLS WITH SHRIMP

8 ounces cream cheese, softened
1/2 onion, minced
1/4 to 1/2 cup sour cream
2 garlic cloves, minced
1 tablespoon lemon juice
1 teaspoon dill weed

1 teaspoon onion salt
1 teaspoon pepper
30 frozen cocktail shrimp, thawed
30 miniature phyllo pastry shells
1 bunch green onions, trimmed and sliced

Preheat the oven to 400 degrees. Combine the cream cheese, onion, sour cream, garlic, lemon juice, dill weed, onion salt, pepper and half the shrimp in a food processor. Process until mixed.

Arrange the pastry shells on a baking sheet and spoon the shrimp mixture evenly into the shells. Bake for 12 to 15 minutes or until bubbly. Cut the remaining 15 shrimp into halves. Top the hors d'oeuvre with equal amount of the shrimp halves and green onions. You may freeze for future use.

Yield: 30 hors d'oeuvre

SCALLOPS EN CROÛTE

3/4 cup white wine

2 teaspoons lemon juice

2 1/2 cups scallops, lightly seared

Salt and pepper to taste

1 onion, sliced

1/4 cup (1/2 stick) butter, softened

2 teaspoons chopped parsley

1 teaspoon grated lemon zest

2 garlic cloves, minced

1 egg, beaten

1 (8-inch) puff pastry round

Preheat the oven to 375 degrees. Mix the wine and lemon juice in a bowl. Add the scallops and stir until coated. Season with salt and pepper and spoon into a 1-quart soufflé dish. Combine the onion, butter, parsley, lemon zest and garlic in a bowl and mix well. Season with salt and pepper and spoon over the scallop mixture.

Brush the edge of the soufflé dish lightly with some of the egg. Top the scallop mixture with the puff pastry, pressing the pastry over the edge of the dish to seal. Brush the surface of the pastry with the remaining egg. Bake for 20 minutes or until puffed and golden brown. Serve immediately.

Yield: 4 servings

CRAB-STUFFED ENDIVE

16 ounces cream cheese, softened

3 pounds snow crab meat, flaked

1 tablespoon lemon juice

1 tablespoon dried dill weed

1 teaspoon salt

4 dashes of hot red pepper sauce

5 ribs celery, chopped

2 or 3 heads Belgian endive,
   separated into spears

Beat the cream cheese in a mixing bowl until smooth, scraping the bowl occasionally. Add the crab meat, lemon juice, dill weed, salt and hot sauce and beat until mixed. Stir in the celery.

Spoon equal amounts of the cream cheese mixture onto the stem end of each endive spear. Garnish with sprigs of dill weed. Serve immediately or chill, covered, for up to 12 hours.

Yield: 2 dozen hors d'oeuvre

Photograph for this recipe appears on page 12.

CHILLED CHICKEN FLORENTINE

Herbed Mayonnaise

1 cup mayonnaise

Juice of 4 lemon wedges

2 teaspoons garlic powder

2 teaspoons oregano

2 teaspoons basil

2 teaspoons rosemary

2 teaspoons paprika

Salt to taste

Chicken and Assembly

4 (6-ounce) boneless skinless chicken breasts

2 bunches fresh spinach, trimmed

3/4 cup white wine

1 1/2 tablespoons rinsed drained capers

1 1/2 tablespoons chopped garlic

4 hard-cooked eggs

For the herbed mayonnaise, mix the mayonnaise, lemon juice, garlic powder, oregano, basil, rosemary, paprika and salt in a bowl. Chill, covered, in the refrigerator.

For the chicken, pound the chicken between sheets of waxed paper on a hard surface until flattened. Sauté the spinach, wine, capers and garlic in a nonstick skillet until the spinach wilts. Remove from the heat and press the excess moisture from the spinach mixture.

Spread the spinach mixture evenly over one side of each chicken breast and place one egg in the center of each. Roll to enclose the eggs and secure with wooden picks. Steam for 10 to 12 minutes or until the chicken is cooked through. Chill, covered, for 2 hours.

Discard the wooden picks and slice each roll into 1/4-inch medallions. Fan the medallions evenly on each of four serving plates and garnish with additional lemon wedges and fresh basil leaves. Serve with the herbed mayonnaise.

Yield: 4 servings

LAMB MEATBALLS WITH YOGURT SAUCE

Lamb Meatballs

1/2 cup bread crumbs

1/4 cup milk

1 pound ground lamb

1 small onion, minced

1/4 cup raisins, minced

1 egg, lightly beaten

2 garlic cloves, minced

Salt and pepper to taste

Yogurt Sauce and Assembly

1 cup plain yogurt

1/4 cup minced scallions

2 tablespoons finely chopped fresh mint

2 tablespoons finely chopped fresh cilantro

1 tablespoon lemon juice

1 tablespoon honey

1 teaspoon freshly grated lemon zest

Dash of salt

For the meatballs, preheat the oven to 350 degrees. Mix the bread crumbs and milk in a bowl and let stand for 5 minutes. Add the ground lamb, onion, raisins, egg, garlic, salt and pepper and mix well. Shape into 1-inch balls and arrange in a baking pan sprayed with nonstick cooking spray. Bake for 35 minutes or until brown and cooked through.

For the sauce, mix the yogurt, scallions, mint, cilantro, lemon juice, honey, lemon zest and salt in a bowl. Serve the meatballs with the sauce for dipping.

Yield: 6 servings

When storing wines, it is important to understand how many elements can negatively affect the taste. Consider the following:

- Air—Exposure to air can cause a wine to quickly turn to vinegar. Store bottles horizontally so the wine stays in contact with the cork.
- Humidity—Proper humidity is important to prevent corks from shrinking. A relative humidity of 70 percent is recommended.
- Light—Light will prematurely age a bottle of wine and give it an unpleasant aroma.
- Odors—Your storage space should be free of any extraneous odors, as they can enter through the cork and contaminate the wine.
- Temperature—A stable storage temperature for wine is in the low- to mid-50s.
- Vibration—Try not to move stored wine until you are ready to drink it.

PINWHEELS

8 ounces cream cheese, softened
1 (10-count) package flour tortillas
20 thin slices honey- and maple-glazed turkey or ham
1 (9-ounce) jar mango chutney, or 1 jar cranberry relish

Spread the cream cheese over one side of each tortilla. Layer each with two slices of the turkey and 3 tablespoons of the chutney. Roll the tortillas to enclose the filling. Wrap each roll in plastic wrap. Chill in the refrigerator.

Trim the ends from the rolls and discard. Cut each roll into six equal slices. Place the pinwheels on a serving platter and garnish with parsley. Or, cover with plastic wrap and store in the refrigerator until serving time. For variety, fill with smoked salmon and capers instead of the turkey and chutney.

Yield: 5 dozen pinwheels

COUNTRY HAM ROLLS

1/2 cup (1 stick) butter
2 tablespoons Champagne mustard
1 small onion, chopped
2 tablespoons poppy seeds
1 teaspoon Worcestershire sauce
1 (32-count) package Parker House rolls
8 slices Swiss cheese
8 slices country ham

Preheat the oven to 350 degrees. Melt the butter in a saucepan and stir in the Champagne mustard, onion, poppy seeds and Worcestershire sauce. Remove the rolls from the foil pan, keeping them together. Cut the rolls horizontally into halves. Return the roll bottoms to the foil pan. Spread the cut sides of the rolls with the butter mixture.

Arrange the cheese and ham evenly over the roll bottoms and top with the roll tops. Cover with foil and bake until heated through. Cut into individual rolls and serve warm.

Yield: 32 rolls

STUFFED MUSHROOMS

12 large mushrooms, stems removed and discarded
1 pound hot bulk pork sausage
8 ounces cream cheese, cubed and softened
1 cup Italian-seasoned bread crumbs
1 teaspoon salt
1/2 teaspoon cayenne pepper
1/4 cup (1/2 stick) butter, melted

Preheat the oven to 400 degrees. Wipe the mushroom caps with a damp cloth. Brown the sausage in a skillet, stirring until crumbly; do not drain. Add the cream cheese, bread crumbs, salt and cayenne pepper and mix well.

Arrange the mushroom caps in a baking dish and fill with the sausage mixture. Drizzle with the butter and bake for 15 minutes. Serve immediately.

Yield: 6 servings

ASPARAGUS HORS D'OEUVRE

A real crowd pleaser, these freeze extremely well and keep for about two months in an airtight container.

24 thin slices white bread, crusts trimmed
4 ounces (about) Gorgonzola cheese or blue cheese, crumbled
8 ounces cream cheese, softened
1 to 2 tablespoons milk (optional)
24 canned or steamed fresh asparagus spears
1/2 to 3/4 cup (1 to 1 1/2 sticks) butter, melted

Flatten the bread slices with a rolling pin until paper-thin. Beat the Gorgonzola cheese and cream cheese in a mixing bowl until creamy, adding enough milk to reach a spreading consistency. Spread the cream cheese mixture over one side of each bread slice and place one asparagus spear on one edge of each slice. Roll to enclose the filling and secure each roll with two wooden picks. Arrange the rolls in a single layer on a baking sheet and freeze until firm.

Preheat the oven to 350 to 375 degrees. Coat the rolls with the butter and cut each roll into three equal portions. Arrange on the baking sheet and bake until golden brown. Discard the wooden picks and serve.

Yield: 6 dozen hors d'oeuvre

BLUE CHEESE BISCUITS

3 tablespoons butter, melted

4 ounces blue cheese, crumbled

1 (10-count) can refrigerator biscuits, cut into quarters

Preheat the oven to 400 degrees. Pour the butter into a 9-inch round baking dish, tilting the dish to ensure even coverage. Sprinkle the cheese over the butter. Arrange the biscuit quarters in a circle beginning at the outer edge and working toward the center. Bake for 11 minutes or until golden brown.

Yield: 6 servings

GREEN CHILE BITES

1/2 cup all-purpose flour

1 teaspoon baking powder

1/4 teaspoon salt

1/2 cup (1 stick) butter

10 eggs

1 pound Cheddar cheese, shredded

4 (4-ounce) cans chopped green chiles

2 cups cottage cheese

Preheat the oven to 400 degrees. Mix the flour, baking powder and salt together. Melt the butter in a 9×13-inch baking dish. Beat the eggs in a mixing bowl until blended. Add the flour mixture, Cheddar cheese, green chiles, cottage cheese and the melted butter and beat until mixed. Pour into the prepared baking dish and bake for 15 minutes.

Reduce the oven temperature to 350 degrees and bake for 35 to 40 minutes longer or until light brown. Cut into 1-inch squares and serve immediately. Reheat before serving, if needed.

Yield: about 90 bites

ROASTED PEPPER BRUSCHETTA

1 head garlic

4 to 5 tablespoons (about) olive oil

1/4 cup balsamic vinegar

1 green bell pepper, cut into 1 1/2-inch strips

1 red bell pepper, cut into 1 1/2-inch strips

1 yellow or orange bell pepper, cut into 1 1/2-inch strips

1 baguette French bread, thinly sliced

Salt to taste

Preheat the oven to 325 degrees. Peel away the papery outer layers of the garlic head, leaving the head intact; do not separate the cloves. Cut off just enough of the top to expose the garlic cloves and brush liberally with some of the olive oil. Place the garlic in a roasting pan or clay garlic roaster. Roast, covered, for 1 hour or until the garlic is very tender.

Heat 2 tablespoons of the remaining olive oil and the balsamic vinegar in a saucepan. Add the bell peppers and simmer over low heat for 50 to 60 minutes or until tender, stirring occasionally.

Brush the baguette slices with the remaining olive oil and sprinkle lightly with salt. Arrange in a single layer on a baking sheet and broil until light brown. If not being served immediately, toast both sides to prevent the slices from becoming soggy. Spread the pulp from 1/2 clove of roasted garlic over each slice. Top with the roasted peppers and serve.

Yield: 8 to 10 servings

TOMATO BASIL BRUSCHETTA

EXECUTIVE CHEF PAUL MATTISON, MATTISON'S™

1 large baguette French bread

2 tablespoons extra-virgin olive oil

4 ripe tomatoes, finely chopped

2 garlic cloves, finely chopped

3 basil leaves, julienned

2 tablespoons extra-virgin olive oil

Pinch of kosher salt

Pinch of cracked pepper

Preheat the oven to 400 degrees. Cut the baguette diagonally into 1/4-inch slices. Brush both sides of the slices with 2 tablespoons olive oil and arrange in a single layer on a baking sheet. Bake for 3 to 5 minutes or until golden brown. You may grill the slices over hot coals, if desired.

Mix the tomatoes, garlic, basil, 2 tablespoons olive oil, the salt and pepper in a bowl. Top each baguette slice with equal amounts of the tomato mixture and garnish with freshly grated Parmigiano-Reggiano cheese.

Yield: 10 servings

CHILI BACON BREADSTICKS

30 thin slices bacon
1/3 cup packed brown sugar
3 tablespoons chili powder
30 crisp breadsticks, broken into halves

Preheat the oven to 350 degrees. Trim the fat from the bacon and cut each slice lengthwise into halves. Mix the brown sugar and chili powder in a shallow dish. Wrap the breadsticks with the bacon and coat with the brown sugar mixture.

Arrange the breadsticks on a rack in a baking pan and bake for 30 to 35 minutes or until the bacon is brown and crisp. Let cool for 15 minutes. Serve at room temperature.

Yield: 5 dozen breadsticks

KAHLÚA PECAN BRIE

1 (15-ounce) round Brie cheese
1/2 cup chopped pecans
2 tablespoons Kahlúa
1 1/2 tablespoons brown sugar

Remove the top rind of the cheese and arrange the round on a serving platter. Heat the pecans, liqueur and brown sugar in a saucepan until the brown sugar dissolves, stirring occasionally. Pour the brown sugar mixture over the cheese. Serve with sliced Granny Smith apples, assorted party crackers and/or gingersnaps.

Yield: 8 servings

GOAT CHEESE APPETIZER

16 ounces goat cheese

8 ounces cream cheese, softened

8 sun-dried tomatoes, chopped

1 tablespoon pesto (optional)

1/2 cup pine nuts, toasted

Line a bowl or mold with plastic wrap, allowing enough overhang to cover the top. Process the goat cheese and cream cheese in a food processor until blended. Add the sun-dried tomatoes and pulse until mixed.

Spoon the goat cheese mixture into the prepared bowl and press lightly. Spread the pesto over the prepared layer and cover with the plastic wrap. Chill for 8 to 10 hours. Invert onto a serving platter, discarding the plastic wrap. Press the pine nuts over the surface. Serve with party crackers.

Yield: 8 servings

MUSHROOM SPREAD

1 garlic clove, minced

1/4 cup (1/2 stick) butter, melted

1 pound mushrooms, thinly sliced or chopped

2 tablespoons parsley flakes, or equivalent
    amount of minced fresh parsley

1 tablespoon dill weed (optional)

1/2 teaspoon salt

1/4 teaspoon pepper

1 cup sour cream

Preheat the oven to 350 degrees. Sauté the garlic in the butter in a saucepan. Stir in the mushrooms. Add the parsley flakes, dill weed, salt and pepper and mix well. Stir in the sour cream. Spoon the mushroom mixture into a baking dish and bake for 45 to 60 minutes or until heated through. Serve warm as a spread with thin crackers or as a side dish. You may freeze for future use. Reheat before serving.

Yield: 20 servings

Red wine and cheese are indelible partners. Why? The proteins in cheese smooth the tannins in red wines. This makes a platter of cheeses and an assortment of red wines the perfect combination for a casual gathering or for the final course of a dinner party. A rule of thumb is that a soft cheese, such as Brie, goes best with pinot noir, whether from France (Burgundy), Oregon, or California, while dry, pressed cheeses pair well with cabernet sauvignon and merlot.

MARIE SELBY BOTANICAL GARDENS

A trip to Sarasota is not complete without a visit to glorious Marie Selby Botanical Gardens. This favorite Sarasota landmark is celebrated for its huge collection of more than 4,900 species of orchids and 3,600 species of bromeliads from around the world. Before your excursion to Selby, start your day with a Lido Frou-Frou and Macadamia Banana French Toast from *Simply Sarasota*.

OYSTER ROLL

1 can smoked oysters, drained
8 ounces cream cheese, softened
1 1/4 tablespoons mayonnaise
1/2 small onion, crushed
1 teaspoon Worcestershire sauce
1 small garlic clove, minced
1/4 teaspoon salt

Mash the oysters in a bowl. Beat the cream cheese and mayonnaise in a mixing bowl until blended. Add the onion, Worcestershire sauce, garlic and salt and beat until mixed.

Cut a sheet of plastic wrap 18 inches long and place on a work surface. Spread the cream cheese mixture into a 5×15-inch rectangle on the plastic wrap. Spoon the oysters down the center of the cream cheese mixture and bring the plastic wrap together to seal. Chill for 24 hours. Garnish with sprigs of parsley and serve with assorted party crackers and/or thin baguette slices. You may freeze for future use.

Yield: 10 servings

SMOKED SALMON SPREAD

8 ounces cream cheese, softened
4 ounces smoked salmon, chopped
1 tablespoon fresh lemon juice
1 tablespoon minced scallion
1 teaspoon chopped fresh dill weed
Pinch of salt
Pinch of pepper

Mix the cream cheese and salmon in a bowl. Stir in the lemon juice, scallion, dill weed, salt and pepper. Chill, covered, for 1 hour. Serve with assorted crackers and/or thinly sliced party bread.

Yield: 8 servings

CRAB CHEESE DIP

8 ounces light cream cheese, softened

1/2 cup light mayonnaise

1/4 cup (1 ounce) grated Parmesan cheese

2 tablespoons skim milk

4 scallions, sliced

1 tablespoon lemon juice

1 teaspoon Tabasco sauce

1 teaspoon Worcestershire sauce

1/2 teaspoon garlic salt

1 pound lump crab meat, flaked

1/4 cup (1 ounce) grated Parmesan cheese

1/4 cup chopped fresh parsley

Preheat the oven to 350 degrees. Combine the cream cheese, mayonnaise, 1/4 cup Parmesan cheese, the skim milk, scallions, lemon juice, Tabasco sauce, Worcestershire sauce and garlic salt in a bowl and mix well. Fold in the crab meat.

Spoon the crab meat mixture into a shallow 6-cup baking dish sprayed with nonstick cooking spray. Sprinkle with 1/4 cup Parmesan cheese. Bake for 30 minutes or until light brown. Let stand for 5 minutes and sprinkle with the parsley. Serve warm with tortilla chips.

Note: Buy extra crab meat for dicing, and sprinkle on top of the dip. Garnish with lemon wedges. Shrimp that has been cooked, peeled, and chopped may be substituted for the crab meat in this dip.

Yield: 8 servings

BLACK BEAN DIP OLÉ

1 (15-ounce) can *Publix* black beans, drained and rinsed

1 cup mild salsa

2 tablespoons chopped onion

2 tablespoons chopped scallions

2 tablespoons chopped fresh cilantro

1 tablespoon lemon juice or lime juice

1 tablespoon olive oil

1 to 2 teaspoons minced garlic

1/4 teaspoon cumin

1 large avocado, chopped

Combine the beans, salsa, onion, scallions, cilantro, lemon juice, olive oil, garlic and cumin in a bowl and mix well. Fold in the avocado just before serving. Serve with tortilla chips and/or pita bread toasts.

Nutrients Per Serving: Cal 108; Prot 3 g; Carbo 14 g; T Fat 7 g; Sat Fat 1 g; Chol 0 mg; Fiber 5 g; Sod 462 mg

Yield: 8 servings

HUMMUS

Homemade hummus is versatile. Just add chopped black olives, sun-dried tomatoes, or spicy peppers for an extra burst of flavor. Serve as a dip for pita chips and crudités, or as a spread for crackers.

1 (19-ounce) can garbanzo beans,
    drained and rinsed
3 green onions, chopped
1/4 cup chopped fresh parsley
2 tablespoons lemon juice
1 tablespoon tahini

3 or 4 garlic cloves
1 teaspoon ground cumin
1/2 teaspoon salt
1/2 teaspoon black pepper
1/8 teaspoon cayenne pepper
1/4 cup olive oil

Combine the beans, green onions, parsley, lemon juice, tahini, garlic, cumin, salt, black pepper and cayenne pepper in a food processor. Add the olive oil gradually, processing constantly until smooth. Serve with pita chips.

Yield: 8 to 10 servings

SOUTHERN-STYLE CAVIAR

1 (16-ounce) can black-eyed peas, drained
1 (16-ounce) can pinto beans, drained
1 (16-ounce) package frozen corn
    kernels, thawed
1 red onion, finely chopped

1 jalapeño chile, finely chopped
1/2 cup vegetable oil
1/2 cup sugar
1/2 cup apple cider vinegar
Salt and pepper to taste

Combine the black-eyed peas, beans, corn, onion and jalapeño chile in a bowl and mix well. Combine the oil, sugar and vinegar in a saucepan and bring to a boil. Boil until the sugar dissolves, stirring occasionally. Let stand until cool.

Pour the vinegar mixture over the bean mixture and mix until coated. Season with salt and pepper. Serve immediately with tortilla chips.

Yield: 8 servings

LEMON DUNK FOR VEGGIES OR SHRIMP

1 cup mayonnaise

1 cup sour cream

1/2 teaspoon salt

1 tablespoon Dijon mustard

1 tablespoon prepared horseradish

Grated zest of 1 lemon

2 tablespoons (or more) lemon juice

Combine the mayonnaise, sour cream, salt, Dijon mustard, horseradish, lemon zest and desired amount of lemon juice in the order listed in a bowl and mix well. Serve with fresh vegetables or shrimp. Store leftovers in the refrigerator.

Yield: 8 servings

MANGO SALSA

Fresh cilantro is always best; the aroma and flavor is worth the extra effort.

2 cups rinsed drained canned black beans

1/2 cup chopped ripe mango

1 small onion, chopped

2 tablespoons chopped red or green bell pepper

2 tablespoons chopped fresh cilantro

2 tablespoons lemon juice or lime juice

1 tablespoon light olive oil

Salt and pepper to taste

Combine the beans, mango, onion, bell pepper, cilantro, lemon juice and olive oil in a bowl and mix well. Season with salt and pepper. Serve with tortilla chips.

Nutrients Per Serving: Cal 64; Prot 3 g; Carbo 14 g; T Fat 2 g; Sat Fat <1 g; Chol 0 mg; Fiber 4 g; Sod 316 mg

Yield: 8 servings

PRALINE DIP

1 1/2 cups chopped pecans
1/4 cup (1/2 stick) butter
1 1/4 cups packed light brown sugar
3/4 cup light corn syrup
3 tablespoons all-purpose flour
1 (5-ounce) can evaporated milk

Preheat the oven to 300 degrees. Spread the pecans in a single layer on a baking sheet and toast for 15 minutes, stirring occasionally. Let stand until cool. Melt the butter in a saucepan and stir in the brown sugar, corn syrup and flour. Bring to a boil and reduce the heat to low.

Simmer for 5 minutes, stirring constantly. Remove from the heat and let stand until lukewarm. Add the evaporated milk and pecans gradually to the brown sugar mixture, stirring constantly. Serve warm with sliced red and green apples for an appetizer, or drizzle over ice cream for dessert.

Yield: 8 to 12 servings

SUN-DRIED TOMATO AND GOAT CHEESE DIP

1/2 cup *Publix* olive oil
36 garlic cloves, julienned
1 (8-ounce) jar sun-dried tomatoes, drained
1 (2-ounce) jar capers
1 teaspoon Italian seasoning
4 ounces chilled goat cheese, coarsely crumbled

Heat the olive oil in a skillet over medium heat and stir in the garlic. Sauté until light brown. Remove from the heat and stir in the sun-dried tomatoes, capers and Italian seasoning.

Pour onto a decorative platter and sprinkle with the cheese. Serve with crisp hardy crackers and/or tortillas. Save preparation time by purchasing garlic cloves in a jar.

Yield: 8 to 10 servings

TAILGATE DIP

3 cups (12 ounces) shredded Cheddar and Monterey Jack cheese
2 fresh tomatoes, peeled and chopped
2 bunches green onions, trimmed and chopped
1 (10-ounce) can tomatoes with green chiles, drained
2 (4-ounce) cans chopped black olives
2 (4-ounce) cans diced green chiles
1 (8-ounce) bottle Italian salad dressing

Combine the cheese, tomatoes, green onions, tomatoes with green chiles, olives, green chiles and salad dressing in a bowl and mix gently. Chill, covered, for 24 hours. Serve with scoop-shaped corn chips.

Yield: 10 servings

Sarasotans love to entertain and many of the grand homes are designed for just that purpose. Here are some favorite tips to use when hosting your next social gathering.

- Place food and drinks in different parts of the room so that you have several conversations and groups happening instead of one large one.
- When making punch, freeze a portion for use as "ice cubes" to keep it well chilled—and not diluted—when it's time to serve.
- When serving buffet-style, plates should be at the front of the line, and silverware and napkins should be at the end. Drinks and desserts should be at a separate table altogether. This will help to avoid juggling too many items while trying to self-serve.
- For a dinner party, slice a stick of butter into 1/2 tablespoon pieces and place on a butter dish. This keeps the dish neat.

SIESTA KEY BREAKFAST SMOOTHIE

Pamper your guests by serving these luscious smoothies in long-stemmed glasses with a chilled sterling silver spoon. Add some bowls of fresh fruit and our Homemade Granola to make a memorable morning meal.

1 cup peach yogurt
1/2 cup orange juice
1 teaspoon honey
1 banana, chopped
4 ice cubes

Combine the yogurt, orange juice, honey, banana and ice cubes in a blender and process until smooth. Pour into long-stemmed glasses and serve immediately. You may substitute 3/4 cup fresh berries for the banana.

Nutrients Per Serving: Cal 145; Prot 4 g; Carbo 29 g; T Fat 2 g; Sat Fat <1 g; Chol 0 mg; Fiber 1 g; Sod 48 mg

Yield: 3 servings

LEMON PUNCH

1 (12-ounce) can frozen lemonade concentrate
2 cups pineapple juice
2 (23-ounce) bottles sparkling mineral water
Lemon slices

Mix the lemonade concentrate, pineapple juice, mineral water and lemon slices in a pitcher and chill. Pour over ice in glasses and serve immediately.

Yield: 9 cups

PARTY PUNCH

1 1/2 cups sugar

1 cup water

4 cups pineapple juice

Juice of 9 oranges (about 2 1/2 cups)

Juice of 6 lemons (about 1 1/4 cups)

1 1/2 cups strong tea

1 (32-ounce) bottle ginger ale, chilled

Combine the sugar and water in a medium saucepan. Cook over medium-high heat until the sugar dissolves, stirring occasionally. Cool slightly and mix with the pineapple juice, orange juice, lemon juice and tea in a large pitcher. Chill in the refrigerator. Add the ginger ale just before serving; do not stir. If serving from a punch bowl, add 1 pint sherbet (lime is good) to the punch after adding the ginger ale and ladle into punch cups.

Yield: 15 to 20 servings

HOT MOCHA WHITE CHOCOLATE

2 ounces white chocolate

1/4 cup half-and-half

3/4 cup freshly brewed hot coffee

Whipped cream

Combine the white chocolate and half-and-half in a saucepan and cook over low heat until heated through, stirring frequently. Or, microwave in a microwave-safe dish until the white chocolate is melted and stir until blended. Pour the white chocolate mixture into a mug and stir in the coffee. Top with a dollop of whipped cream and serve.

Yield: 1 serving

SMASHING SANGRIA

This elegant drink is an obvious choice for a party, especially when served from brightly colored pitchers. Have fun with dinner guests and serve this as a welcome drink when they first arrive in your home. Send each guest home with the recipe to remember your time together.

2 gallons burgundy

1 gallon orange juice

4 liters Seven-Up

4 liters Sprite

3 cups sugar

2 (6- to 8-ounce) jars maraschino cherries

6 oranges, sliced

2 cinnamon sticks

Combine the burgundy, orange juice, Seven-Up, Sprite, sugar, cherries, oranges and cinnamon sticks in a 10-gallon container and mix well. Let stand at room temperature for 1 hour. Discard the cinnamon sticks. For a smaller crowd, decrease the amounts.

Yield: 40 servings

BLONDE SANGRIA

1 (750-milliliter) bottle white wine (chardonnay or riesling)

1 cup pineapple juice

1 (7-ounce) bottle lemon-lime soda

1/3 cup orange juice

1/4 cup sugar

3 tablespoons lemon juice

1 tablespoon lime juice

Orange slices

Mix the wine, pineapple juice, soda, orange juice, sugar, lemon juice, lime juice and orange slices in a pitcher. Pour over ice in glasses and serve.

Yield: 8 servings

LIDO FROU-FROU

1 tablespoon grenadine, chilled
1/3 cup sparkling water, lemon-lime soda or Champagne, chilled
1/4 cup orange juice, chilled
2 tablespoons peach or apricot nectar, chilled

Pour the grenadine into a stemmed goblet. Add enough sparkling water to fill the glass halfway. Add enough orange juice to almost fill the glass and top off with the nectar. Garnish with a skewer of mandarin oranges and raspberries.

Nutrients Per Serving: Cal 98; Prot 1 g; Carbo 24 g; T Fat <1 g; Sat Fat <1 g; Chol 0 mg; Fiber <1 g; Sod 8 mg

Yield: 1 serving *Photograph for this recipe appears on the back cover.*

POINSETTIAS

This festively titled beverage is a beauty for the holidays and a good substitute for traditional eggnog. Garnish with cranberries and a sprig of mint for a beautiful, aromatic presentation.

Sugar
3 cups cranberry juice cocktail
3 cups Champagne
1/2 cup orange liqueur

Moisten the rims of eight glasses with water. Dip the rims in sugar and rotate gently to cover the rims evenly. Mix the cranberry juice cocktail, Champagne and liqueur in a pitcher and pour into the prepared glasses.

Yield: 8 servings

Madame Pompadour described it as the only wine leaving a woman still beautiful after drinking it. Voltaire exclaimed that the bubbles reflected the soul of France. And the monk Dom Perignon is said to have exclaimed after testing his experiment, "I am drinking stars!" We're speaking of Champagne, of course. True Champagne comes only from a relatively small area north of Paris. By French law, that name cannot be used to describe other sparkling wines. While true Champagne is usually superb, other sparklers can be brilliant, too. Try Cava from Spain, Sekt from Germany, and a whole host of California sparkling wines. And, while a bubbly is wonderful as an aperitif, for a very special occasion serve it throughout the meal. Salut!

MARGARITAS

1 (6-ounce) can frozen limeade concentrate
1/2 cup tequila
1/2 cup Triple Sec
Juice of 1 lemon
Ice

Combine the limeade concentrate, tequila, liqueur, lemon juice and ice in a blender and process until blended. Pour into margarita glasses and serve.

Serves 3

WHISPERS

Whispers first appeared in Fare by the Sea, *the Junior League of Sarasota's 1983 cookbook. This magical after-dinner coffee drink was invented at the Whispering Sands Inn, once located on Siesta Key. Although the Inn is long gone, the recipe was shared with the founders of the Field Club, a favorite Sarasota location, and has been a specialty of the club ever since.*

1 quart coffee ice cream
1/2 ounce brandy
1/2 ounce crème de cocoa

Pack enough of the ice cream into a blender to fill three-fourths full. Add the brandy and liqueur and process until of a liquid consistency. Pour the ice cream mixture into a freezer container and freeze until firm. Serve in small goblets.

Serves 4 to 6

Espresso Martinis

1/4 cup whipping cream, chilled
6 tablespoons vodka
6 tablespoons Kahlúa or other coffee liqueur
1/4 cup freshly brewed espresso or double-brewed coffee, chilled
Ice cubes

Whisk the whipping cream in a medium bowl just until thickened. Combine the vodka, liqueur, espresso and ice in a cocktail shaker and shake well. Strain the martinis evenly into two martini glasses. Top with the whipped cream and serve.

Yield: 2 servings

White Cosmo

2 1/2 ounces vodka
1 ounce Triple Sec
2 ounces white cranberry juice
1/2 ounce fresh Key lime juice
Ice

Combine the vodka, liqueur, cranberry juice, lime juice and ice in a cocktail shaker and shake until chilled. Strain into glasses. Garnish each with two or three fresh cranberries and serve.

Nutrients Per Serving: Cal 149; Prot <1 g; Carbo 11 g; T Fat <1 g; Sat Fat <1 g; Chol 0 mg; Fiber <1 g; Sod 2 mg

Yield: 2 servings

This may be the South, but if you're looking for tea cakes and mint juleps, you've come too far south. Sarasota residents don't spend a lot of time perched primly on the edges of their chairs sipping weak tea. They are folks who live with gusto and seriously relax, often with a cool glass of wine, a brew, or a cocktail. They love their martinis and will shake just about any concoction with ice and pour it into a martini glass. How can you get that colored sugar to stick to the rim of the glass? Rub the rim of a cocktail glass with a lemon or lime wedge; dip the glass into a shallow dish of sugar, so that the sugar sticks to only the rim.

Basil Breakfast Strata, page 50

Simply
Rising

BREADS
& BRUNCH

CHOCOLATE CHERRY BANANA BREAD

2 cups all-purpose flour

1 teaspoon baking soda

1/4 teaspoon salt

1/2 cup (1 stick) butter, softened

1 cup packed brown sugar

2 eggs

2 teaspoons vanilla extract

2 cups mashed bananas (2 or 3 bananas)

1 teaspoon ground cinnamon

1/2 teaspoon freshly grated or ground nutmeg

1/4 cup sour cream

3/4 cup each chocolate chips and dried cherries

Preheat the oven to 350 degrees. Mix the flour, baking soda and salt together. Beat the butter and brown sugar in a mixing bowl until creamy, scraping the bowl occasionally. Add the eggs one at a time, beating well after each addition. Stir in the vanilla. Add the bananas, cinnamon and nutmeg and beat until blended. Add the flour mixture and sour cream alternately, beating well after each addition. Fold in the chocolate chips and cherries. Spoon the batter into a buttered 4×8-inch loaf pan and bake for 1 hour or until a wooden pick inserted in the center comes out clean. Cool in the pan for 10 minutes. Remove to a wire rack to cool completely.

Yield: 10 servings

BLUEBERRY BREAD

3 cups unbleached all-purpose flour

2 teaspoons cream of tartar

1 teaspoon baking soda

1/2 teaspoon each ground cinnamon, ground nutmeg and ground cloves

1/2 teaspoon salt

1 pint blueberries

1 cup sugar

1 cup milk

1/3 cup butter

1 egg, beaten

1/2 teaspoon lemon extract

Preheat the oven to 375 degrees. Sift the flour, cream of tartar, baking soda, cinnamon, nutmeg, cloves and salt into a bowl and mix well. Combine 1/3 cup of the flour mixture with the blueberries in a bowl and toss until coated. Beat the sugar, milk, butter, egg and flavoring in a mixing bowl until creamy, scraping the bowl occasionally. Add the remaining flour mixture and beat until blended. Fold in the blueberries. Spoon the batter into two 4×8-inch loaf pans sprayed with nonstick cooking spray. Bake for 30 to 35 minutes or until a wooden pick inserted in the centers comes out clean. Cool in the pans for 10 minutes. Remove to a wire rack to cool completely. You may substitute well-drained frozen blueberries for the fresh blueberries.

Nutrients Per Serving: Cal 182; Prot 3 g; Carbo 32 g; T Fat 5 g; Sat Fat 3 g; Chol 25 mg; Fiber 1 g; Sod 189 mg

Yield: 16 servings

DATE AND NUT BREAD

2 cups boiling water
4 cups chopped dates
2 cups walnuts pieces
4 cups all-purpose flour
2 teaspoons baking soda

1 teaspoon salt
1 1/2 cups packed brown sugar
1/2 cup shortening
2 eggs

Preheat the oven to 350 degrees. Pour the boiling water over the dates and walnuts in a bowl. Mix the flour, baking soda and salt together. Beat the brown sugar and shortening in a mixing bowl until creamy, scraping the bowl occasionally. Add the eggs and beat until blended. Add the flour mixture and date mixture alternately, beating well after each addition and adding additional water if the batter is too stiff.

Spoon the batter into two 5×9-inch loaf pans sprayed with nonstick cooking spray. Bake for 45 minutes. Cool in the pans for 10 minutes. Remove to a wire rack to cool completely. You may bake in four miniature loaf pans for 30 minutes.

Yield: 16 servings

RAISIN BRAN MUFFINS

3 3/4 cups Raisin Bran cereal
2 1/2 cups all-purpose flour
1 1/2 cups granulated sugar
2 1/2 teaspoons baking soda
2 cups buttermilk

1/2 cup vegetable oil
2 eggs, beaten
1/4 cup chopped dates
3/4 cup Grape-Nuts cereal
1/4 cup packed brown sugar

Preheat the oven to 400 degrees. Combine the Raisin Bran, flour, granulated sugar and baking soda in a bowl and mix well. Stir in the buttermilk, oil, eggs and dates. Spoon into muffin cups sprayed with nonstick cooking spray.

Combine the Grape-Nuts cereal and brown sugar in a bowl and mix well. Sprinkle evenly over the top of the batter. Bake for 15 minutes. Cool in the pans for 2 minutes and remove to a wire rack to cool completely.

Yield: about 20 muffins

IRISH SODA BREAD WITH RAISINS

1 cup raisins	3/4 teaspoon baking powder
Bailey's Irish cream	3/4 teaspoon baking soda
3 cups all-purpose flour	1/2 teaspoon salt
1/4 cup sugar	1 1/2 cups plain yogurt
1 teaspoon caraway seeds	

Mix the raisins with enough liqueur to cover in a bowl. Let stand at room temperature for 8 to 10 hours.

Preheat the oven to 375 degrees. Mix the flour, sugar, caraway seeds, baking powder, baking soda and salt in a bowl. Stir in the raisin mixture and yogurt and knead briefly. Shape the dough into a round loaf on a baking sheet. Cut a large X in the top of the loaf and bake for 45 minutes or until golden brown.

Yield: 12 to 16 servings

MEXICAN CORN BREAD

1 (17-ounce) can cream-style corn	1 teaspoon sugar
1 cup buttermilk	1/2 teaspoon salt
1/2 cup vegetable oil	1 (4-ounce) can chopped green chiles,
2 eggs, beaten	drained, or to taste
1/2 cup all-purpose flour	1 1/2 cups (6 ounces) shredded sharp
1/2 cup cornmeal	Cheddar cheese
2 teaspoons baking powder	

Preheat the oven to 350 degrees. Coat a 9-inch cast-iron skillet with a small amount of oil and heat in the oven for 5 minutes. Combine the corn, buttermilk, 1/2 cup oil and the eggs in a bowl and mix well. Mix the flour, cornmeal, baking powder, sugar and salt in a bowl and stir into the corn mixture.

Pour half the batter into the hot skillet and sprinkle with the green chiles and 3/4 cup of the cheese. Top with the remaining batter and sprinkle with the remaining 3/4 cup cheese. Bake for 45 to 50 minutes or until brown and crisp. Cut into wedges and serve.

Yield: 8 wedges

BACON CHEDDAR SCONES

LATITUDE 23.5 FINE COFFEE AND TEA

4 slices bacon, chopped
3 cups all-purpose flour
1 tablespoon baking powder
1 tablespoon sugar
1 1/2 teaspoons salt
1/2 cup (1 stick) unsalted butter, chopped
1 1/2 cups (6 ounces) shredded sharp Cheddar cheese
1/2 cup thinly sliced green onions
1/2 teaspoon freshly ground pepper
1 cup plus 2 tablespoons heavy cream

Preheat the oven to 400 degrees. Cook the bacon in a skillet until brown and crisp; drain. You may microwave the bacon until crisp, if desired. Sift the flour, baking powder, sugar and salt together into a bowl. Cut the butter, cheese, green onions and pepper into the flour mixture with a pastry blender or fork just until the mixture begins to form lumps. Add the bacon. Add 1 cup of the heavy cream and mix just until the dough becomes sticky; do not overwork.

Turn the dough onto a lightly floured surface and shape into a ball. Divide the dough into two equal portions and shape each portion into a 7-inch round, 3/4 inch thick. Cut each round into eight wedges using a sharp knife. Arrange the wedges 1/2 inch apart on a baking sheet. Brush the tops with the remaining 2 tablespoons heavy cream and bake for 22 to 23 minutes or until golden brown. Cool slightly and serve.

Yield: 16 scones

ALMOND COFFEE CAKE

This coffee cake freezes and defrosts well, so make several at once. It is always nice to have one on hand for an easy and elegant treat.

3/4 cup (1 1/2 sticks) butter or margarine, melted	Pinch of salt
1 1/2 cups sugar	1 teaspoon almond extract
2 eggs	3 to 4 ounces slivered almonds
1 1/2 cups sifted all-purpose flour	1 to 2 teaspoons sugar

Preheat the oven to 350 degrees. Line a 9- or 11-inch cast-iron skillet with foil, allowing enough overhang to cover the coffee cake. Combine the butter and 1 1/2 cups sugar in a mixing bowl and beat until blended. Add the eggs one at a time, beating well after each addition. Beat in the flour, salt and flavoring.

Spoon the batter into the prepared skillet and sprinkle with the almonds and 1 to 2 teaspoons sugar. Bake for 30 to 40 minutes or until the coffee cake tests done. Use the foil to remove the coffee cake to a wire rack and let stand until cool. Wrap tightly in the foil to store. Do not try to remove the foil while the coffee cake is warm as it will stick. You may bake in a buttered and floured 9-inch cake pan.

Yield: 8 servings

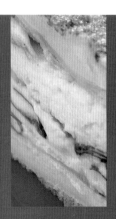

Coffee Tips

- Always start with the freshest whole bean coffee available.
- Purchase only the amount of coffee beans that you will use in a week. Coffee gets stale—and you can taste the difference. Store your coffee in an airtight package in a cool, dry location.
- Buy a coffee grinder! Grinding your coffee beans just before brewing imparts incomparable flavor.
- Sample different single-estate coffees and different coffee blends and appreciate how coffee grown in different regions and altitudes under very different conditions can taste radically different.
- Remember that coffee is mostly water; use only good-quality filtered water in your brew.

Blitz Kuchen (German Coffee Cake)

1 1/2 cups cake flour

1 teaspoon baking powder

1 cup sugar

1/4 cup shortening

2 egg yolks

1/4 teaspoon salt

1/2 cup milk

2 egg whites

3 tablespoons butter, melted

Cinnamon and sugar to taste

Preheat the oven to 350 degrees. Sift the cake flour and baking powder together. Beat the sugar and shortening in a mixing bowl until creamy. Add the egg yolks and salt and beat until blended. Add the cake flour mixture and milk alternately, beating well after each addition.

Beat the egg whites in a mixing bowl until stiff peaks form; fold into the batter. Spoon the batter into a greased and floured 9×9-inch baking pan and drizzle with the butter. Sprinkle with cinnamon and sugar and bake for 30 minutes. You may freeze for future use.

Yield: 9 servings

Monkey Bread

1 cup finely chopped nuts

3/4 cup granulated sugar

1 1/2 teaspoons ground cinnamon

3 (10-count) cans refrigerator buttermilk biscuits

1 cup granulated sugar

3/4 cup (1 1/2 sticks) butter

1/4 cup packed brown sugar

1 teaspoon ground cinnamon

1/4 cup evaporated milk

Preheat the oven to 350 degrees. Mix the nuts, 3/4 cup granulated sugar and 1 1/2 teaspoons cinnamon in a shallow dish. Cut the biscuits into quarters and coat with the nut mixture. Place in a greased bundt pan.

Mix 1 cup granulated sugar, the butter, brown sugar, 1 teaspoon cinnamon and the evaporated milk in a saucepan and bring to a boil. Boil until the sugar dissolves, stirring occasionally. Pour over the biscuit quarters and bake for 45 to 55 minutes or until light brown.

Yield: 10 to 12 servings

Simply Sarasota

CANOPY WALK →

MYAKKA RIVER STATE PARK

When you ask visitors where the best place to picnic is, they inevitably mention the nearby well-known beaches. When you ask a local, the answer is Myakka River State Park. The park offers many picnicking spots along the river's edge, in the hammock forests, and, of course, at the picnic tables. On your next picnic, try the recipes for Pinwheels and Sarasota Summer Salad for starters. Make a "Florida" finish with Key Lime Cake, all from the pages of *Simply Sarasota*.

MACADAMIA BANANA FRENCH TOAST

Macadamia nuts are indigenous to Hawaii, so decorate your table to resemble the tropics with orchids or birds of paradise. To make bowls, cut pineapples and coconuts into halves and scoop out the pulp.

8 to 10 slices dry white bread or French bread

1 cup milk

1 banana, cut into quarters

4 eggs

1 (3-ounce) jar macadamia nuts, crushed

1 teaspoon vanilla extract

Dash of ground cinnamon or nutmeg

Confectioners' sugar to taste

2 bananas, sliced

Preheat the oven to 475 degrees. Arrange the bread slices in a single layer in one or two dishes. Butter two large baking sheets generously. Combine the milk, banana quarters, eggs, half the macadamia nuts, the vanilla and cinnamon in a blender or food processor and process until blended. Pour over the bread slices and let stand until saturated. Turn to coat the remaining sides.

Arrange the slices in a single layer on the prepared baking sheets. Bake for 5 minutes per side or until golden brown, turning once. Dust with confectioners' sugar and top with the sliced bananas and the remaining macadamia nuts.

Yield: 8 to 10 slices

OVERNIGHT MAPLE FRENCH TOAST

1/2 cup (1 stick) butter

1 cup packed brown sugar

2 tablespoons maple syrup

2 tablespoons chopped pecans

12 (1-inch) slices French bread

1 1/2 cups milk or half-and-half

5 eggs

1 teaspoon vanilla extract

1/2 teaspoon rum extract, or

   1 tablespoon dark rum (optional)

1/4 teaspoon salt

Confectioners' sugar

Melt the butter in a saucepan and stir in the brown sugar and maple syrup. Add the pecans and mix well. Spread over the bottom of a 9×13-inch baking pan sprayed with nonstick cooking spray. Arrange the bread slices in a single layer over the brown sugar mixture. Whisk the milk, eggs, flavorings and salt in a bowl until blended and pour over the bread slices. Chill, covered, for 8 hours or longer.

Preheat the oven to 350 degrees. Bake, uncovered, for 45 minutes or until light brown. Dust with confectioners' sugar. Serve with warm maple syrup and whipped cream.

Yield: 12 slices

ARTICHOKE QUICHE

1 unbaked (9-inch) pie shell
2 (6-ounce) jars marinated artichokes
1 small onion, finely chopped
1 garlic clove, minced
4 eggs
1/4 cup dry bread crumbs

1/8 teaspoon oregano
1/8 teaspoon Tabasco sauce
8 ounces sharp Cheddar cheese, shredded
2 tablespoons finely chopped fresh parsley
Salt and pepper to taste

Preheat the oven to 400 degrees. Bake the pie shell for 10 minutes; set aside. Reduce the oven temperature to 325 degrees. Drain the artichokes, reserving the marinade. Sauté the onion and garlic in the reserved marinade in a skillet for 5 minutes.

Whisk the eggs in a bowl until blended. Stir in the bread crumbs, oregano and Tabasco sauce. Add the artichokes, onion mixture, cheese, parsley, salt and pepper. Pour into the pie shell and bake for 45 minutes. Serve warm. You may freeze for future use.

Yield: 6 to 8 servings

CRUSTLESS CRAB QUICHE

4 *Publix* eggs, beaten
1 cup sour cream
1 cup small curd cottage cheese
1/2 cup (2 ounces) grated Parmesan cheese
1/4 cup all-purpose flour
1 teaspoon onion powder
1/4 teaspoon salt

4 drops of Tabasco sauce
6 ounces fresh, frozen or canned lump
    crab meat, flaked
2 cups (8 ounces) shredded Monterey
    Jack cheese
3 or 4 cans mushrooms, drained

Preheat the oven to 350 degrees. Combine the eggs, sour cream, cottage cheese, Parmesan cheese, flour, onion powder, salt and Tabasco sauce in a food processor fitted with a metal blade. Process until blended and pour into a large bowl. Fold in the crab meat, Monterey Jack cheese and mushrooms.

Pour the crab meat mixture into a 9- or 10-inch porcelain or glass pie plate. Bake for 45 minutes or until a knife inserted in the center comes out clean and the top is puffed and golden brown. Let stand for 5 minutes before cutting into wedges. You may substitute cooked ham or cooked sausage for the crab meat, as well as add broccoli or spinach.

Yield: 8 servings

BASIL BREAKFAST STRATA

Basil Pesto

2 cups fresh basil leaves

1 cup walnuts

1 cup olive oil

1 cup (4 ounces) freshly grated
    Parmesan cheese

1/4 cup (1 ounce) freshly grated
    Romano cheese

4 garlic cloves

Pinch of salt

Pinch of pepper

Strata

1 cup milk

1/2 cup dry white wine

1 (16-ounce) loaf French bread,
    cut into 1/2-inch slices

2 cups fresh spinach leaves

Olive oil

8 ounces cooked ham, sliced

1 pound Havarti cheese, sliced

3 tomatoes, sliced

4 eggs, beaten

Pinch of salt

Pinch of pepper

1/2 cup heavy cream

For the pesto, combine the basil, walnuts, olive oil, Parmesan cheese, Romano cheese, garlic, salt and pepper in a food processor and process to the desired consistency. You may substitute commercially prepared pesto for the homemade pesto.

For the strata, mix the milk and wine in a shallow dish. Dip the bread slices in the milk mixture and squeeze the slices lightly to remove any excess liquid. Arrange the bread slices in a single layer in a 10×13-inch baking dish.

Dip the spinach in olive oil; drain. Layer the ham, spinach, cheese, tomatoes and pesto one-half at a time in the order listed over the bread slices. Whisk the eggs, salt and pepper in a bowl until blended and pour over the prepared layers. Chill, covered, for 8 to 10 hours.

Preheat the oven to 350 degrees. Bring the strata to room temperature and pour the heavy cream over the top. Bake for 45 to 60 minutes or until the strata tests done. Serve warm.

Yield: 8 to 10 servings   *Photograph for this recipe appears on page 38.*

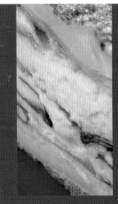

Peeling Boiled Eggs
After draining hot water, bang the eggs around inside the pan to crack the shells, and then fill the pan with cold water. The water will get under the shells and cool the eggs quickly, allowing the shells to be removed easily.

VEGETABLE BRUNCH BAKE

Pasteurized egg substitute equivalent to
   10 eggs
1/2 cup all-purpose flour
1/4 cup (1/2 stick) butter
1 1/2 teaspoons onion powder
1 teaspoon garlic powder
1 teaspoon baking powder

3 cups low-fat cottage cheese
3 cups (12 ounces) shredded Cheddar cheese
2 cups chopped sun-dried tomatoes
10 ounces spinach, chopped
1 bunch green onions, chopped
1/2 red bell pepper, chopped
1/2 yellow bell pepper, chopped

Preheat the oven to 350 degrees. Combine the egg substitute, flour, butter, onion powder, garlic powder, baking powder and 1 cup of the cottage cheese in a blender or food processor and process until blended.

Pour the egg substitute mixture into a bowl and stir in the remaining cottage cheese, the Cheddar cheese, sun-dried tomatoes, spinach, green onions and bell peppers. Divide the cheese mixture evenly between two greased 10-inch baking dishes and bake for 40 to 45 minutes or until set.

Nutrients Per Serving: Cal 311; Prot 24 g; Carbo 17 g; T Fat 16 g; Sat Fat 10 g; Chol 45 mg; Fiber 3 g; Sod 590 mg

Yield: 12 servings

BREAKFAST PIZZA

1 (8-count) can refrigerator crescent rolls
1 pound bulk pork sausage
1 1/2 cups Southwestern hash brown potatoes
2 cups (8 ounces) shredded sharp
   Cheddar cheese

4 eggs
1/4 cup milk
Pinch of salt
Pinch of pepper
1/4 cup (1 ounce) grated Parmesan cheese

Preheat the oven to 350 degrees. Unroll the crescent roll dough and separate into rectangles. Press over the bottom and partially up the sides of a 9×13-inch baking pan, pressing the edges and perforations to seal.

Brown the sausage in a skillet, stirring until crumbly. Drain and cool. Layer the sausage, potatoes and Cheddar cheese in the order listed in the prepared baking pan. Whisk the eggs, milk, salt and pepper in a bowl until blended. Pour over the prepared layers and sprinkle with the Parmesan cheese. Bake for 25 to 28 minutes or until golden brown. Let stand for 10 minutes before serving. You may freeze for future use.

Yield: 6 to 8 servings

CHEESY HASH BROWNS

These are a great accompaniment to roast beef or beef tenderloin, but the color enhances any entrée.

2 pounds hash brown potatoes

2 cups (8 ounces) shredded Cheddar cheese

1 (10-ounce) can cream of chicken soup

1 (10-ounce) can cream of mushroom soup

1 1/2 cups sour cream or nonfat sour cream

1/2 cup chopped onion

1/2 cup (1 stick) butter, melted

1 teaspoon salt

Dash of pepper

2 cups crushed cornflakes

1/4 cup (1/2 stick) butter, melted

Preheat the oven to 350 degrees. Combine the potatoes, cheese, soups, sour cream, onion, 1/2 cup butter, the salt and pepper in a bowl and mix well. Spoon the potato mixture into a greased 9×13-inch baking pan.

Toss the cornflakes with 1/4 cup butter in a bowl until coated. Sprinkle over the prepared layer. Bake for 1 hour. Serve warm.

Yield: 12 to 16 servings

HOMEMADE GRANOLA

5 cups old-fashioned oats

1 cup wheat germ

1/3 cup olive oil

1/2 cup packed brown sugar

2 tablespoons light corn syrup

1 teaspoon vanilla extract

1/2 cup raisins

1/2 cup sunflower seeds

1/2 cup nuts

1/2 cup dried cranberries

1/2 cup shredded coconut

1/2 cup (3 ounces) chocolate chips or
   butterscotch chips

1/2 cup dried pineapple chunks

Preheat the oven to 300 degrees. Mix the oats and wheat germ in a large bowl. Combine the olive oil, brown sugar, corn syrup and vanilla in a saucepan and mix well. Cook until the brown sugar dissolves, stirring occasionally. Pour the olive oil mixture over the oat mixture and toss to coat. Spread the oat mixture on a baking sheet and bake for 30 minutes. Let stand until cool.

Toss the oat mixture with the raisins, sunflower seeds, nuts, cranberries, coconut, chocolate chips and/or pineapple chunks in a bowl. Store in jars with tight-fitting lids or in sealable plastic bags. You may freeze the granola for future use. Substitute with your favorite dried fruits and nuts.

Yield: 20 servings

FRUIT PUFF PASTRIES

1 (17-ounce) package frozen puff pastry, thawed
1/3 cup all-fruit peach or apricot spread
1 teaspoon finely shredded lemon zest
1 cup finely chopped peeled peaches (about 2 peaches)
1 cup blueberries
8 ounces cream cheese, softened
1/4 cup packed brown sugar
1 teaspoon vanilla extract
1/4 cup confectioners' sugar

Cut the pastry into 2×4-inch rectangles or any desired shape using cookie cutters. Arrange the pastry rectangles in a single layer on a baking sheet and bake using the package directions until golden brown. Remove to a wire rack to cool. Cut the rectangles into halves.

Heat the peach spread in a saucepan until melted and stir in the lemon zest. Let cool slightly and fold in the peaches and blueberries. Beat the cream cheese, brown sugar and vanilla in a mixing bowl until creamy.

Spread 1 to 2 tablespoons of the cream cheese mixture over the centers of half the puff pastry squares. Layer with a spoonful of the peach mixture. Top with the remaining puff pastry squares. Sift the confectioners' sugar over the tops and serve immediately.

Note: These must be eaten immediately after assembly; otherwise, they get soggy. However, you can make each part separately ahead of time. The cream cheese mixture and the peach mixture will last in the refrigerator for a few days. The puff pastries will stay fresh for several hours in an airtight container at room temperature. Do not refrigerate the puff pastries, however.

Yield: 8 servings

Summer Corn and Black Bean Salad, page 78

Simply *Fresh*

MEDITERRANEAN SEAFOOD STEW

1/4 cup olive oil

1 cup chopped leek

1/2 cup minced fennel bulb

6 to 8 garlic cloves, minced

2 (14-ounce) cans low-sodium chicken broth

1 (28-ounce) can crushed tomatoes

3 (8-ounce) bottles clam juice

1/2 cup Grand Marnier

1/2 orange

1 teaspoon dried basil

1 teaspoon dried thyme

2 bay leaves

2 pounds large shrimp, peeled

2 pounds cod, cut into 1 1/2-inch pieces

1 1/2 pounds sea scallops

1 pound mussels, rinsed

Heat the olive oil in a large saucepan and stir in the leek, fennel and garlic. Cook for 5 minutes, stirring occasionally. Add the broth, tomatoes, clam juice, liqueur, orange, basil, thyme and bay leaves. Bring to a boil and reduce the heat to low.

Simmer, covered, for 30 minutes. Discard the orange and bay leaves. Stir in the shrimp, cod, scallops and mussels. Simmer for 5 to 7 minutes or until the fish is firm and the mussels have opened; discard any unopened mussels. Ladle into soup bowls and garnish each serving with minced fresh basil.

Nutrients Per Serving: Cal 515; Prot 69 g; Carbo 18 g; T Fat 14 g; Sat Fat 2 g; Chol 269 mg; Fiber 3 g; Sod 947 mg

Yield: 8 servings

PASTA FAGIOLI

1 pound ground pork

1 small onion, chopped

1 small garlic clove, minced

2 cups chicken broth

1 (16-ounce) can white beans, navy beans or
    Great Northern beans

1 (14-ounce) can Italian-style chopped tomatoes

1/2 cup small pasta shells or macaroni

1/4 cup sherry or white wine

1/2 teaspoon each crushed fennel seeds and
    black pepper

1/4 teaspoon each crushed red pepper and salt

Brown the ground pork in a large saucepan, stirring until crumbly; drain. Stir in the onion and garlic and cook until the onion is tender. Add the broth, beans, tomatoes, pasta, sherry, fennel seeds, black pepper, red pepper and salt and mix well.

Bring to a boil and reduce the heat to low. Simmer for 10 to 12 minutes or until the pasta is tender, stirring occasionally. Ladle into soup bowls and serve immediately. You may freeze the soup for future use.

Yield: 4 servings

ARTICHOKE AND ANDOUILLE SOUP

1 pound smoked andouille or smoked sausage,
   casings removed and sausage coarsely chopped
3 yellow, green and/or red bell peppers, coarsely chopped
1 cup coarsely chopped onion
1/4 cup (1/2 stick) butter
4 1/2 tablespoons all-purpose flour
5 to 6 cups half-and-half
1 (14-ounce) can artichoke hearts, drained and mashed
1 cup (4 ounces) shredded Pepper Jack cheese
1 cup vermouth
2 tablespoons Worcestershire sauce
1 cup chicken broth
1 tablespoon basil
1 1/2 teaspoons oregano
3 dashes of Tabasco sauce, or to taste
1/8 teaspoon ground red pepper
1/8 teaspoon black pepper

Process the sausage, bell peppers and onion in a food processor until finely chopped; do not liquefy the vegetables. Melt the butter in a Dutch oven or stockpot. Sauté the sausage mixture in the butter and stir in the flour, half-and-half, artichokes, cheese, vermouth, Worcestershire sauce and broth. Add the basil, oregano, Tabasco sauce, red pepper and black pepper and mix well.

Simmer for 30 minutes, stirring frequently to prevent the cheese from scorching. Ladle into soup bowls and serve immediately. You may freeze the soup for future use.

Yield: 8 servings

CHICKEN CORN CHOWDER

8 ounces bacon, chopped

1 pound boneless skinless chicken breasts, cut into bite-size pieces

2 ribs celery, chopped

1 large onion, chopped

6 cups chicken broth

3 cups heavy cream

2 potatoes, peeled and chopped

1 (12-ounce) package frozen corn kernels

1 teaspoon thyme

Salt and pepper to taste

Cook the bacon in a Dutch oven over medium-high heat until crisp. Add the chicken and cook until the chicken is cooked through, stirring frequently. Stir in the celery and onion and cook for 10 minutes or until the vegetables are tender. Add the broth, heavy cream, potatoes, corn, thyme, salt and pepper and mix well.

Simmer until the potatoes are tender and the chowder is of the desired consistency, stirring occasionally. Ladle into soup bowls and serve immediately.

Note: Serve as a warm and comforting starter; top with chopped peppers and spicy cheese to add zest.

Yield: 6 to 8 servings

CHICKEN LIME CHILI

1 small onion, chopped

3 garlic cloves, chopped

1/2 jalapeño chile, chopped

1 teaspoon ground red pepper

1/2 teaspoon ground cumin

1 teaspoon olive oil

2 (15-ounce) cans Great Northern beans

1 (14-ounce) can chicken broth

1 (4-ounce) can green chiles, chopped

1 tomato, chopped

1 teaspoon chili powder

8 ounces chopped cooked chicken breasts

Juice of 2 large limes

Sauté the onion, garlic, jalapeño chile, red pepper and cumin in the olive oil in a large saucepan for 5 minutes. Stir in the beans, broth, green chiles, tomato and chili powder. Bring to a boil and boil for 5 minutes. Reduce the heat to low.

Simmer for 10 minutes, stirring occasionally. Stir in the chicken and simmer for 4 minutes. Stir in the lime juice and cook for 1 minute. Ladle into chili bowls.

Nutrients Per Serving: Cal 257; Prot 21 g; Carbo 35 g; T Fat 4 g; Sat Fat 1 g; Chol 30 mg; Fiber 8 g; Sod 595 mg

Yield: 6 servings

WHITE CHILI

For a hearty and attractive meal, serve this in sourdough bread bowls—no clean up necessary!

8 boneless skinless chicken breasts, chopped
1 1/2 pounds onions, chopped
1/4 cup corn oil
4 cups warm water
2 (4-ounce) cans diced green chiles
1 cup salsa
1 1/2 tablespoons oregano
1 tablespoon salt
3 1/2 teaspoons ground cumin

2 1/2 teaspoons garlic powder
2 teaspoons parsley flakes
1 teaspoon ground red pepper
4 chicken bouillon cubes
5 (15-ounce) cans Great Northern beans or
    navy beans
Sour cream
Shredded Cheddar cheese

Cook the chicken and onions in the corn oil in a 12-quart stockpot over medium heat for 15 minutes, stirring frequently. Stir in the warm water, green chiles, salsa, oregano salt, cumin, garlic powder, parsley flakes, red pepper and bouillon cubes. Bring to a boil and reduce the heat to low.

Simmer for 15 minutes, stirring occasionally. Stir in the beans and cook for 15 minutes longer. Let stand for 15 minutes before ladling into chili bowls. Top each serving with sour cream and cheese.

Yield: 12 to 16 servings

Gathering more than one pattern of china to set an eclectic table is an artistic opportunity that's sure to be a lively topic of conversation when your guests sit down. To visually and aesthetically maximize this style of tabletop décor, consider some simple guidelines. The same background color of the china will help bring together a diverse grouping. Avoid mixing ivory and white backgrounds. Plate patterns should have a unifying element: a gold or silver border or botanical designs, or have a dominant color or scene. If you're combining silver patterns too, keep each place setting intact, rather than using a knife from one pattern and spoon from another. Using the same color napkins for all the place settings will also ensure overall harmony, but napkins rings can be varied.

TURKEY CHILI

KEVIN HALL, DIRECTOR OF BRAND, FIRST WATCH RESTAURANTS

1 yellow onion, chopped

1 jalapeño chile, seeded and chopped

1 pound ground turkey

1 (6-ounce) can tomato paste

1/4 cup chili powder

1 tablespoon ground cumin

1 cup chicken stock

1 (4-ounce) chopped green chiles

4 plum tomatoes, chopped

1 bunch cilantro, trimmed and chopped

Sauté the onion and jalapeño chile in a 4-quart nonstick saucepan. Add the ground turkey and cook until the ground turkey is brown and crumbly, stirring frequently. Stir in the tomato paste and cook for 2 minutes. Add the chili powder and cumin and cook for 1 minute. Stir in the stock and reduce the heat to low.

Add the green chiles, tomatoes and cilantro to the ground turkey mixture and simmer for 20 minutes, stirring occasionally. Ladle into chili bowls and serve immediately.

Nutrients Per Serving: Cal 199; Prot 18 g; Carbo 14 g; T Fat 8 g; Sat Fat 2 g; Chol 55 mg; Fiber 4 g; Sod 740 mg

Yield: 6 servings

ONION SOUP

6 yellow onions, chopped

1/2 cup light olive oil

1 (25-ounce) bottle dry red wine

1 teaspoon dried thyme, crushed

1 large bay leaf

4 (10-ounce) cans beef consommé

5 cups water

1 loaf French bread, cut into 1/2-inch slices

6 cups (24 ounces) shredded Swiss cheese

Sauté the onions in the olive oil in a Dutch oven until tender. Stir in the wine, thyme and bay leaf. Bring to a boil and boil for 5 minutes. Stir in the consommé and water and reduce the heat to low.

Simmer for 20 minutes, stirring frequently. Discard the bay leaf and ladle the soup into heatproof soup bowls. Top each serving with one slice of bread and about 1/2 cup of the cheese. Arrange the bowls on a baking sheet and broil for 2 to 3 minutes or until the cheese is melted.

Yield: 8 to 12 servings

CREAMY GREENS SOUP

1 onion, chopped
2 ribs celery, chopped
1 tablespoon vegetable oil
4 cups vegetable or chicken stock
1 cup split peas
1 bay leaf

2 cups vegetable or chicken stock
2 zucchini, chopped
1 (16-ounce) package frozen chopped
   spinach
1 teaspoon Italian seasoning
Salt and pepper to taste

Cook the onion and celery in the oil in a stockpot over medium-high heat until tender, stirring frequently. Add 4 cups stock, the peas and bay leaf and mix well. Reduce the heat to low.

Simmer for 40 minutes or until the peas are tender, stirring occasionally. Discard the bay leaf and stir in 2 cups stock and the zucchini. Cook until the zucchini is very tender. Process the zucchini mixture in a blender or with a handheld immersion blender until puréed. Return the purée to the stockpot and stir in the spinach and Italian seasoning.

Simmer for 5 minutes or until the spinach is tender. Add additional stock or water if a thinner consistency is desired. Season with salt and pepper and ladle into soup bowls. You may substitute an equivalent amount of water and bouillon cubes for the stock. You may freeze the soup for future use.

Nutrients Per Serving: Cal 143; Prot 9 g; Carbo 23 g; T Fat 3 g; Sat Fat <1 g; Chol 0 mg; Fiber 9 g; Sod 764 mg

Yield: 8 servings

TOMATO BACON SOUP

1 pound *Publix* center-cut bacon, sliced
1 large onion, chopped
1 bell pepper, chopped
1 rib celery, chopped

4 garlic cloves, minced
4 (14-ounce) cans diced tomatoes
1 cup cream
Salt and pepper to taste

Sauté the bacon in a heavy stockpot just until the bacon begins to brown. Drain, reserving 2 tablespoons of the bacon drippings. Add the onion, bell pepper, celery and garlic to the reserved bacon mixture and cook over medium-high heat until the vegetables turn golden brown, stirring frequently. Stir in the tomatoes and simmer for 20 minutes.

Stir in the cream and simmer for 5 minutes. Blend the soup until smooth using a handheld immersion blender, or process in batches in a blender or food processor. Reheat, if necessary. Season with salt and pepper. Ladle into soup bowls.

Yield: 6 to 8 servings

FRENCH VEGETABLE SOUP

1 zucchini

1 large, or 2 small, leek bulbs,
  rinsed and thinly sliced

3 tablespoons butter

3 carrots, peeled and sliced

4 red potatoes, peeled and
  cut into 3/4-inch pieces

2 small turnips, peeled and cut into 3/4-inch
  pieces (optional)

6 cups vegetable stock or chicken stock

1 cup dry white wine

1/2 cup half-and-half

Salt and pepper to taste

Cut the zucchini horizontally into halves and cut each half into slices. Cook the leeks in the butter in a stockpot over medium heat until tender. Stir in the carrots, potatoes and turnips. Cook for 3 minutes, stirring occasionally.

Add the stock and wine and mix well. Simmer, covered, until the potatoes and carrots are tender-crisp. Stir in the zucchini and cook until tender. Mix in the half-and-half and simmer just until heated through, stirring occasionally. Season with salt and pepper and ladle into soup bowls. You may substitute an equivalent amount of water and bouillon cubes for the stock.

Nutrients Per Serving: Cal 265; Prot 5 g; Carbo 37 g; T Fat 8 g; Sat Fat 5 g; Chol 22 mg; Fiber 4 g; Sod 1040 mg

Yield: 6 servings

COOL CUCUMBER SOUP

3/4 cup chopped green onions

6 tablespoons butter

6 cups chicken broth

4 1/2 cups chopped cucumbers

1 cup (heaping) chopped potatoes

1 1/2 cups watercress leaves

Salt and pepper to taste

3 cups sour cream

Tabasco sauce to taste

Sauté the green onions in the butter in a large saucepan until tender. Stir in the broth, cucumbers and potatoes. Simmer for 15 minutes, stirring occasionally. Add the watercress and season with salt and pepper.

Process the cucumber mixture in a blender until puréed. Chill, covered, in the refrigerator. Stir in the sour cream and Tabasco sauce and ladle into soup bowls.

Yield: 10 to 11 servings

MANGO SOUP

This delectable chilled soup is made with two of Sarasota's favorite homegrown fruits, mangoes and oranges. Beautiful in color, this dish is as pleasing to the eye as it is delicious—perfect fare for Florida's summer months.

3 ripe mangoes, peeled and chopped
Zest of 1 orange, or 1 tablespoon grated orange zest
1 1/2 cups buttermilk
1 cup orange juice
1 tablespoon honey
Pinch of seasoned salt
Lime juice or lemon juice to taste

Process the mangoes and orange zest in a blender or food processor until mixed. Spoon into a bowl and chill, covered, for 24 hours. Stir the mango mixture and blend in the buttermilk, orange juice, honey, seasoned salt and lime juice. Ladle into soup bowls and garnish with chopped or sliced naval oranges and/or mint leaves.

Yield: 6 to 8 servings

Given Sarasota's tropical climate and enthusiasm for *al fresco* entertaining, chilled soups should be far more popular than they are. You can change that. Presented as a first course or as a refreshingly original dessert, cold soups should be as pretty to look at as they are tasty. First-course soups rely on intriguing combinations of puréed vegetables, such as Cool Cucumber Soup. Many dessert soups start with bases of yogurt, cream, or fresh fruit concentrates to build layers of tantalizing flavors. Consider Mango Soup served in an oversized martini glass with a colorful garnish—that would invigorate anyone's taste buds. Remember to search your pantry for unusual or unexpected vessels in which to serve your chilled soup, because this course just might be the "Wow!" factor your guests remember.

SALADE AUX CHAMPIGNONS

1 large garlic clove

1 teaspoon salt

1/4 teaspoon pepper

1/4 teaspoon rosemary

1/4 teaspoon tarragon

Pinch of curry powder

1 1/2 tablespoons wine vinegar

1/4 cup olive oil

4 ounces fresh mushrooms, sliced

2 tablespoons chopped fresh parsley

1 head French endive, separated into spears

3 heads Bibb lettuce, trimmed and separated into leaves

1 head Boston lettuce, trimmed and separated into leaves

Spinach leaves

Combine the garlic with salt in a bowl and mash until the garlic is crushed. Combine the pepper, rosemary, tarragon and curry powder in a bowl and stir in the vinegar. Add the olive oil and mix until incorporated. Stir in the mushrooms and parsley. Let stand at room temperature for 30 minutes or longer.

Toss the endive, lettuces and spinach in a salad bowl. Add the mushroom mixture and crushed garlic mixture and toss to mix. Serve immediately.

Nutrients Per Serving: Cal 115; Prot 3 g; Carbo 7 g; T Fat 9 g; Sat Fat 1 g; Chol 0 mg; Fiber 4 g; Sod 413 mg

Yield: 6 servings

MATTISON'S™ HOUSE SALAD

EXECUTIVE CHEF PAUL MATTISON, MATTISON'S™

1 cup balsamic vinegar
1 egg yolk
2 tablespoons chopped shallots
1 tablespoon chopped garlic
2 tablespoons chopped fresh basil
3 cups olive oil
1/2 cup (2 ounces) grated Parmigiano-Reggiano cheese
6 to 10 ounces salad greens
2 tomatoes, chopped
Crumbled Gorgonzola cheese to taste
Toasted pine nuts to taste

Purée the vinegar, egg yolk, shallots and garlic in a blender Add the basil. Add the olive oil gradually, processing constantly until the olive oil is incorporated. Add the Parmigiano-Reggiano cheese and process to blend.

Drizzle the dressing over the salad greens in a salad bowl, tossing to coat. Top with the tomatoes, Gorgonzola cheese and pine nuts. Serve immediately.

Note: If you are concerned about using raw egg yolks, use yolks from eggs pasteurized in their shells, which are sold at some specialty food stores, or use an equivalent amount of pasteurized egg substitute.

Yield: 8 servings

Don't be afraid to jazz up a packaged salad with fresh herbs or kick up a jar of salsa with fresh cilantro and jalapeño chiles. To make seedless jalapeño chile rings: First, cut off the stem end of the jalapeño chile. Then, insert a vegetable peeler into the chile cavity and twirl it around to remove the ribs and seeds. Shake the remaining seeds out of the chile. Finally, slice it into rings.

THE JOHN & MABLE RINGLING MUSEUM OF ART

From the "Greatest Show on Earth" to the greatest home in Sarasota . . . John and Mable Ringling lived and built their dream house, Cà d'Zan, on Sarasota Bay. The house was started in 1924 and completed by 1926 and was built with entertaining in mind. Ron McCarty, who has worked at the John and Mable Ringling Museum for twenty-five years, says it was rumored that John kept a tank of turtles in his basement to provide the turtle soup that was one of his favorite dishes. Guests dined on one of the many beautiful china patterns in the collection the Ringlings owned, which included a 500-piece set of Cantagalli earthenware from Florence, Italy.

SARASOTA SUMMER SALAD

Parsley Vinaigrette

1/4 cup vegetable oil

2 tablespoons sugar

2 tablespoons white vinegar

1 tablespoon parsley

1/2 teaspoon salt

Dash of black pepper

Dash of hot red pepper sauce

Salad

1/2 head Boston lettuce, trimmed and torn into
   bite-size pieces

1/2 head red leaf lettuce, trimmed and torn
   into bite-size pieces

1 quart fresh strawberries, sliced

1/2 cup slivered almonds

1 (11-ounce) can mandarin oranges, drained

For the vinaigrette, combine the oil, sugar, vinegar, parsley, salt, black pepper and hot sauce in a jar with a tight-fitting lid and shake to mix.

For the salad, toss the lettuces, strawberries, almonds and mandarin oranges in a salad bowl. Add the vinaigrette and toss to coat. Serve immediately.

Yield: 6 servings

BACON AND ALMOND SALAD

Dijon Vinaigrette

1/2 cup olive oil

1/4 cup sugar

1/4 cup chopped onion

2 tablespoons red wine vinegar

1 tablespoon Dijon mustard or
   honey mustard

Salad

6 to 10 ounces mixed salad greens

4 slices crisp-cooked bacon, drained and
   crumbled, or equivalent amount of
   bacon bits

6 ounces sliced almonds or cashews, toasted

Cherry tomatoes, sliced

For the vinaigrette, whisk the olive oil, sugar, onion, vinegar and Dijon mustard in a bowl until thickened; do not chill.

For the salad, toss the salad greens, bacon, almonds and tomatoes in a salad bowl. Add the vinaigrette and toss to coat.

Yield: 6 servings

SWISS CASHEW TOSSED SALAD

Poppy Seed Dressing

1 cup vegetable oil
3/4 cup sugar
1/3 cup white vinegar
1 tablespoon grated red onion
2 teaspoons prepared mustard
1 teaspoon poppy seeds
Dash of salt

Salad

1 head romaine, torn
4 ounces Swiss cheese, julienned
1 cup salted cashew halves

For the dressing, combine the oil, sugar, vinegar, onion, prepared mustard, poppy seeds and salt in a jar with a tight-fitting lid and shake to mix.

For the salad, toss the romaine, cheese and cashews in a salad bowl. Add the dressing and toss to coat.

Yield: 4 to 6 servings

Known as the Circus King, John Ringling promoted Sarasota in many ways. He was a business partner of Owen Burns, and together they planned and developed some of Sarasota's most well-known sites and landmarks, including the Ringling Causeway Bridge, St. Armand's Key, Bird Key, Coon Key, and 2,000 acres on Longboat Key.

AUTUMN SALAD

Fall is short-lived in Sarasota. Enjoy this fabulous, colorful salad bursting with seasonal flavors as often as possible.

Apple Cider Vinaigrette

1/2 cup vegetable oil
1/4 cup sugar
3 tablespoons apple cider vinegar
1/4 teaspoon salt

Salad

4 cups spring mix
1 pear, sliced or chopped
4 ounces blue cheese, crumbled
1/2 cup dried cranberries
1/4 cup pecans, toasted

For the vinaigrette, combine the oil, sugar, vinegar and salt in a jar with a tight-fitting lid and shake to mix.

For the salad, toss the spring mix, pear, cheese, cranberries and pecans in a salad bowl. Add the vinaigrette and toss to coat. Serve immediately.

Yield: 4 to 6 servings

ROMAINE AND WALNUT SALAD

6 tablespoons olive oil
2 teaspoons Dijon mustard
1 1/2 teaspoons sugar
8 cups torn romaine

1 large Granny Smith apple, cut into
  bite-size pieces
2 to 3 tablespoons crumbled blue cheese
2 tablespoons chopped walnuts

Whisk the olive oil, Dijon mustard and sugar in a large salad bowl until blended. Add the lettuce and toss until coated. Sprinkle with the apple, cheese and walnuts and mix until combined. Serve immediately.

To prepare in advance, toss the lettuce with the oil mixture and cover with a damp paper towel. Place the blue cheese and walnuts on the paper towel. Slice the apple just before serving.

Yield: 8 servings

JAPANESE GINGER SALAD

1 cup vegetable oil

1/3 cup soy sauce

1/3 cup white vinegar

1/4 cup sesame seeds

3 tablespoons minced fresh ginger

1 small onion, chopped

1/2 rib celery, chopped

1 teaspoon sugar

1 teaspoon ketchup

5 cups mixed salad greens

Combine the oil, soy sauce, vinegar, sesame seeds, ginger, onion, celery, sugar and ketchup in a blender or food processor and process until smooth. Drizzle the dressing over the salad greens in a salad bowl and toss to coat. Serve immediately.

Yield: 8 servings

STEAK SALAD

1 (4- to 6-ounce) filet mignon

Salt and cracked pepper to taste

5 cups *Publix* packaged salad greens

1 cup dried cherries

1/2 cup sliced Vidalia onion

1/2 cup crumbled blue cheese or
   Roquefort cheese

1/3 cup chopped walnuts

Vinaigrette

Preheat the broiler. Season the filet with salt and cracked pepper. Arrange the filet on a broiler rack and broil to the desired degree of doneness; medium-rare is suggested. Let stand until cool and cut into diagonal slices.

Toss the filet, salad greens, cherries, onion, cheese and walnuts in a salad bowl. Add the desired amount of vinaigrette and toss to coat. Serve immediately.

Yield: 4 to 6 servings

WILD RICE SHRIMP SALAD

1 pound unpeeled shrimp

1 (6-ounce) package long grain and
    wild rice mix

1 (7-ounce) jar marinated artichokes

4 green onions, sliced

1/2 cup chopped green bell pepper

1/4 cup sliced celery

1/3 cup mayonnaise

3/4 teaspoon curry powder

Leaf lettuce

Cook the shrimp in boiling water in a large saucepan for 3 to 5 minutes or until the shrimp turn pink; drain. Rinse the shrimp with cold water and peel. Reserve six of the whole shrimp and chop the remaining shrimp. Cook the rice using the package directions. Drain and chop the artichokes, reserving 3 tablespoons of the marinade.

Combine the chopped shrimp, rice, artichokes, green onions, bell pepper and celery in a bowl and mix well. Mix the reserved artichoke marinade, mayonnaise and curry powder in a bowl until blended and stir into the shrimp mixture. Chill, covered, for 5 hours. Spoon the shrimp salad onto lettuce-lined plates or into a lettuce-lined salad bowl and top with the reserved whole shrimp.

Yield: 6 servings

PASTA NIÇOISE

Flavored olive oils provide a great variation. Try the lemon olive oil fresh from Saturday morning's Farmer's Market in downtown Sarasota.

Dijon Vinaigrette

3 tablespoons red wine vinegar or
    sherry vinegar

1 tablespoon creamy Dijon mustard

1/3 cup olive oil

Salad

1 pound pasta, cooked and drained

1 pound fresh green beans, steamed

1 (12-ounce) can water-pack albacore
    tuna, drained

4 or 5 tomatoes, chopped

1 bunch green onions, finely chopped

2 tablespoons fresh lemon juice

For the vinaigrette, whisk the vinegar and Dijon mustard in a bowl until blended. Add the olive oil gradually, whisking constantly until the oil is incorporated.

For the salad, toss the pasta, beans, tuna, tomatoes and green onions in a bowl. Add the vinaigrette and lemon juice and toss to coat.

Yield: 12 servings

COBB PASTA SALAD

Honey Dijon Dressing

1 cup olive oil

1/4 cup red wine vinegar

1 garlic clove, minced

1 teaspoon honey

1 teaspoon Dijon mustard

1/2 teaspoon pepper

Salad

16 ounces wagon wheel pasta

2 cups chopped cooked chicken (rotisserie or boiled)

2 cups fresh spinach leaves, shredded

10 ounces bacon, crisp-cooked and crumbled

1 cup black olives

4 ounces blue cheese or feta cheese, crumbled

2 ripe tomatoes, chopped

For the dressing, combine the olive oil, vinegar, garlic, honey, Dijon mustard and pepper in a jar with a tight-fitting lid and shake to mix.

For the salad, cook the pasta using the package directions until al dente. Drain and rinse. Toss the pasta, chicken, spinach, bacon, olives, cheese and tomatoes in a large salad bowl. Add the dressing and mix gently until coated.

Yield: 8 to 10 servings

- Quick Peel Tomatoes: Drop tomatoes into boiling water for 15 to 30 seconds. Remove from water with slotted spoon and peel. The skin will come right off using your fingertips.
- Seed Tomatoes: Slice in half and squeeze each half while shaking downward to remove liquid and seeds. Remove the remaining seeds using your fingers.
- Tomato Paste: Open both ends of the can and push entire contents into a plastic sandwich bag and freeze. Remove from the bag and slice into 1/4 inch rounds (one tablespoon each). Put all rounds back into plastic bag and freeze, then use portions as needed.

CHICKEN PASTA SALAD VERONIQUE

Creamy Lemon Dressing

3/4 cup mayonnaise

2 tablespoons fresh lemon juice

Salt and pepper to taste

Salad

4 cups chopped cooked chicken breasts
  (2 1/2 large chicken breasts)

2 cups cooked elbow macaroni

1 1/2 cups red or green seedless grape halves
  (8 ounces)

4 ounces blue cheese, crumbled

1/2 cup sliced almonds, toasted

1 tablespoon chopped fresh chives

For the dressing, mix the mayonnaise and lemon juice in a bowl. Season with salt and pepper.

For the salad, toss the chicken, pasta, grapes, cheese and almonds in a salad bowl. Fold the dressing into the chicken mixture and chill, covered, in the refrigerator. Sprinkle with the chives just before serving. You may prepare up to one day in advance and store, covered, in the refrigerator.

Yield: 4 entrée servings, or 6 to 8 luncheon servings

ASIAN CHICKEN PASTA SALAD

16 ounces spaghetti
1 rotiserrie chicken
1/2 cup soy sauce
1/4 cup olive oil
1/4 teaspoon chili oil
1 cup light mayonnaise
1 tablespoon Dijon mustard
3/4 teaspoon Oriental sesame oil

1/2 to 1 tablespoon chili oil
1 (10-ounce) package frozen peas
 (do not thaw)
1 red bell pepper, chopped
1/2 to 1 cup shredded carrots
3/4 cup chopped snow peas
3/4 cup chopped fresh cilantro

Cook the pasta using the package directions. Drain and let stand until cool. Chop the chicken into bite-size pieces, discarding the skin and bones.

Toss the pasta, soy sauce, olive oil and 1/4 teaspoon chili oil in a bowl. Mix the mayonnaise, Dijon mustard, sesame oil and 1/2 to 1 tablespoon chili oil in a bowl. Add the mayonnaise mixture to the pasta mixture and mix well. Stir in the chicken, frozen peas, bell pepper, carrots, snow peas and cilantro. Chill, covered, until serving time. The flavor of the salad is enhanced if prepared one day in advance and stored, covered, in the refrigerator.

Yield: 8 to 10 servings

ORZO SALAD

16 ounces orzo
1/4 cup olive oil
1 (10-ounce) package frozen baby
 green peas, thawed
1 red bell pepper, chopped
1 green bell pepper chopped
3/4 cup chopped green onions

1 (4-ounce) can chopped black olives
1/4 cup chopped green olives
2/3 cup balsamic vinegar
3 tablespoons teriyaki sauce
1 tablespoon soy sauce
10 ounces feta cheese, crumbled

Cook the pasta using the package directions and drain. Add the olive oil to the pasta and toss to coat. Stir in the peas, bell peppers, green onions and olives.

Whisk the vinegar, teriyaki sauce and soy sauce in a bowl until blended. Add the vinegar mixture to the pasta mixture and toss to coat. Chill, covered, until serving time. Adjust the seasonings. Sprinkle with the cheese just before serving.

Yield: 12 servings

TOMATO BASIL PASTA SALAD

16 ounces farfalle

1/4 cup olive oil

2 garlic cloves, minced

4 fresh basil leaves, coarsely chopped

4 plum tomatoes, sliced

1 cup (4 ounces) grated Parmigiano-Reggiano
    cheese or asiago cheese

Cook the pasta using the package directions. Drain and rinse with cold water. Toss the pasta, olive oil, garlic and basil in a salad bowl until combined. Stir in the tomatoes and sprinkle with the cheese. This is a great vegetarian entrée but is also good topped with grilled chicken or shrimp.

Yield: 4 to 6 servings

ORIENTAL SALAD

Salad

2 tablespoons butter

1 (3-ounce) package ramen noodles, broken
    (discard flavor packet)

2 tablespoons sesame seeds

1 ounce slivered almonds

1 tablespoon sugar

1/2 (12-ounce) package broccoli slaw

1/2 (16-ounce) package cabbage slaw

2 green onions, sliced

Oriental Dressing

1/3 cup vegetable oil

1/4 cup sugar

4 to 6 tablespoons red wine vinegar

3 tablespoons soy sauce

For the salad, melt the butter in a skillet and stir in the noodles, sesame seeds and almonds. Cook for 5 minutes or until the almonds are light brown, stirring constantly. Stir in the sugar and cook for 1 minute longer. Spoon the noodle mixture onto a plate to cool. Toss the noodle mixture, broccoli slaw, cabbage slaw and green onions in a salad bowl.

For the dressing, combine the oil, sugar, vinegar and soy sauce in a jar with a tight-fitting lid and shake to mix. Add the dressing to the salad mixture just before serving and toss to coat.

Yield: 8 servings

CRANBERRY AND WALNUT SLAW

Celery Seed Dressing
1/3 cup cider vinegar
1/3 cup vegetable oil
1/3 cup sugar
1 teaspoon celery seeds

Salad
2 cups shredded red cabbage
2 cups shredded green cabbage
1 cup coarsely chopped walnuts
1 cup dried cranberries
1/3 cup thinly sliced red onion

For the dressing, combine the vinegar, oil, sugar and celery seeds in a jar with a tight-fitting lid and shake to mix.

For the salad, toss the cabbage, walnuts, cranberries and onion in a salad bowl. Add the dressing and toss to coat. Chill, covered, for about 3 hours. Just before serving, stir the salad and drain any excess dressing. Store, covered, in the refrigerator for up to 5 days.

Yield: 6 to 8 servings

Charles Ringling, brother of John, also lived in Sarasota. He owned a mansion, on forty acres just north of Cà d'Zan, made of pink marble and linked by a portico to a smaller house built for his daughter, Hester. Many of the best dinner parties and social events of that time period were held at either Cà d'Zan or Charles Ringling's home.

CHICK-PEA AND FETA SALAD

Lemon Dijon Dressing
1/2 cup olive oil

1/3 cup fresh lemon juice

2 teaspoons Dijon mustard

1 1/2 teaspoons salt

1 teaspoon basil oil

1/4 teaspoon freshly ground pepper

Salad
2 (20-ounce) cans chick-peas, drained

1 red onion, chopped

8 ounces feta cheese, crumbled

2 tablespoons chopped fresh parsley

For the dressing, combine the olive oil, lemon juice, Dijon mustard, salt and basil oil in a jar with a tight-fitting lid and shake to mix.

For the salad, toss the chick-peas, onion and dressing in a bowl until coated. Chill, covered, for 1 hour or longer. Just before serving stir in the cheese and parsley. Serve on a lettuce-lined platter garnished with fresh basil leaves.

Yield: 10 servings

SUMMER CORN AND BLACK BEAN SALAD

Lime Dressing
1/3 cup olive oil

Juice of 1 lime

2 teaspoons ground cumin

1 teaspoon salt

1 teaspoon pepper

Salad
1 (14-ounce) can black beans, drained and rinsed

2 cups frozen corn kernels

2 tomatoes, chopped

1 red bell pepper, chopped

1 small purple onion, chopped

1/2 cup fresh cilantro, chopped

For the dressing, combine the olive oil, lime juice, cumin, salt and pepper in a jar with a tight-fitting lid and shake to mix.

For the salad, combine the beans, corn, tomatoes, bell pepper, onion and cilantro in a salad bowl and mix gently. Pour the dressing over the bean mixture and let stand for 30 minutes or longer. Toss and serve.

Note: When refrigerated, this actually gets better with time. After a day or two, drain it in a colander and serve over romaine lettuce, in a four-cheese tortilla, or with chips. Add avocado just before serving for extra richness.

Yield: 6 to 8 servings

Photograph for this recipe appears on page 54.

ZESTY CUCUMBER SALAD

2 cucumbers, peeled
3 tablespoons apple cider vinegar
1 tablespoon vegetable oil

1 teaspoon sugar
Salt and pepper to taste

Slice the cucumbers lengthwise into halves and remove the seeds. Thinly slice each half. Combine the vinegar, oil, sugar, salt and pepper in a bowl and mix well. Add the cucumbers to the vinegar mixture and mix well. Serve immediately or chill, covered, in the refrigerator.

For **Asian Cucumber Salad**, add $1/4$ cup sliced scallions, 1 tablespoon sesame oil and 1 teaspoon soy sauce to the vinegar mixture.

For **Swedish Cucumber Salad**, add $1/4$ cup minced fresh dill weed to the vinegar mixture.

Nutrients Per Serving: Cal 32; Prot <1 g; Carbo 2 g; T Fat 2 g; Sat Fat <1 g; Chol 0 mg; Fiber <1 g; Sod 2 mg
Nutritional profile does not include the variations.

Yield: 6 servings

CREAMY CUCUMBER SALAD

3 English cucumbers, peeled and sliced
1 large white or Vidalia onion, thinly sliced
   and separated into rings (optional)
3 tablespoons salt
1 cup sour cream

2 tablespoons white vinegar
$1 1/2$ tablespoons sugar
2 garlic cloves, chopped
$1/4$ teaspoon white pepper
Hungarian paprika to taste

Toss the cucumbers, onion and salt in a bowl. Chill, covered, for 2 to 10 hours. Drain and press the excess moisture from the cucumbers and onion. Combine the cucumber mixture, sour cream, vinegar, sugar, garlic and white pepper in a serving bowl and mix gently. Sprinkle with paprika and serve immediately.

Yield: 4 servings

WASABI POTATO SALAD

8 red potatoes, quartered

Salt to taste

1/4 cup olive oil

2 tablespoons lime juice

1 tablespoon sesame oil

1 tablespoon rice wine vinegar or
   white wine vinegar

1 teaspoon sugar

1 teaspoon wasabi powder

1 cup sliced celery

1/2 cup minced scallions

1/4 cup minced fresh cilantro

Cook the potatoes in boiling salted water in a saucepan until fork tender. Drain and let stand until cool. Whisk the olive oil, lime juice, sesame oil, vinegar, sugar and wasabi powder in a bowl until blended. Add the potatoes, celery, scallions and cilantro to the oil mixture and toss until coated. Chill, covered, until serving time.

Yield: 8 to 10 servings

CAPRESE SALAD

2 pints cherry tomatoes, cut into halves

4 ounces fresh mozzarella cheese,
   cut into 1/4-inch cubes

1/3 cup sliced green olives

1/3 cup chopped fresh basil

2 tablespoons balsamic vinegar

1 tablespoon olive oil

Toss the tomatoes, cheese, olives, basil, vinegar and olive oil in a bowl until coated. Chill, covered, until serving time.

Note: For an hors d'oeuvre, layer ingredients on a toothpick: Pierce a grape tomato, followed by a fresh basil leaf and a small cube of mozzarella. Drizzle olive oil and red wine vinegar over the serving tray before passing.

Nutrients Per Serving: Cal 170; Prot 7 g; Carbo 11 g; T Fat 12 g; Sat Fat 5 g; Chol 22 mg; Fiber 2 g; Sod 395 mg

Yield: 4 servings

CRANBERRY SALAD

2 cups sugar
2 cups water
1 (16-ounce) package fresh cranberries
1 (6-ounce) package cherry gelatin
1 cup English walnuts, coarsely chopped
1 (16-ounce) can crushed pineapple

Mix the sugar and water in a saucepan and bring to a boil. Boil for 5 minutes. Stir in the cranberries and return to a boil. Boil for 5 minutes, stirring occasionally. Remove from the heat.

Add the gelatin and stir until dissolved. Stir in the walnuts and pineapple and pour into a 9×13-inch dish. Chill until set.

Yield: 12 to 15 servings

When tasting wines, you should first examine its color. Is it clear, hazy or opaque? Next, take a deep sniff. Swirl the wine to allow aromas to escape as the wine "opens up" in the glass. Does it smell like fruit? Flowers? Pepper? Now take a drink. Swish it around in your mouth, sensing not only its taste but also its texture and weight, or "mouth feel." As the moment of that first tasting changes to the wine gently cascading down your throat, let the memory of the wine on your palate "speak" to your own taste. The aftertaste, or "finish," of a wine can be brief or lengthy, extraordinary or off-putting, but is usually a major influence in our ultimate enjoyment of a favorite wine. Savor it in each sip.

Caribbean Rice, page 84

Simply Complementary

BARLEY AND MUSHROOM CASSEROLE

1/2 cup (1 stick) butter or margarine

1 cup quick-cooking barley

1 onion, chopped

2 cups chicken broth

1/2 cup slivered almonds

1 (2-ounce) envelope onion soup mix

1 (3-ounce) can sliced mushroom, or

   1 cup sliced fresh mushrooms

Butter to taste

1 (5-ounce) can sliced water chestnuts

Preheat the oven to 350 degrees. Melt 1/2 cup butter in a saucepan and stir in the barley and onion. Sauté until light golden brown. Remove from the heat and stir in the broth, almonds and soup mix.

Drain the canned mushrooms, reserving the liquid. Sauté the mushrooms in butter in a skillet until tender. Stir the reserved mushroom liquid, sautéed mushrooms and water chestnuts into the barley mixture. Pour into a 2-quart baking dish and bake, covered, for 1 hour, adding additional liquid if needed. You may prepare one to two days in advance and store, covered, in the refrigerator. Bake just before serving. You may freeze leftovers for future use.

Yield: 6 servings

CARIBBEAN RICE

This dish works well as a stand-alone meal, but try it as a side dish for pork and the results will be rewarding.

2 cups hot cooked rice

1 (11-ounce) can mandarin oranges, drained

1 (8-ounce) can crushed pineapple

1/2 cup chopped red bell pepper

1/2 cup slivered almonds, toasted

1/2 cup grated unsweetened coconut

1/3 cup chopped green onions

2 tablespoons hot mango chutney

1/4 teaspoon ground ginger

Combine the rice, mandarin oranges, pineapple, bell pepper, almonds, coconut, green onions, chutney and ginger in a large skillet and mix well. Cook over medium-high heat until heated through, stirring frequently. Serve immediately.

Yield: 6 servings

Photograph for this recipe appears on the front cover and on page 82.

ORZO

8 ounces orzo

1/2 cup extra-virgin olive oil

1 red bell pepper, chopped

1 yellow bell pepper, chopped

1 orange bell pepper, chopped

1 red onion, chopped

2 carrots, chopped

8 sun-dried tomatoes, chopped

20 kalamata olives, cut into halves

1/4 cup (1 ounce) freshly grated
   Parmesan cheese

3 or 4 garlic cloves, minced

1/2 teaspoon kosher salt

1/4 cup (1 ounce) freshly grated
   Parmesan cheese

Cook the pasta using the package directions until al dente and drain. Cover to keep warm. Heat the olive oil in a large skillet and stir in the bell peppers, onion, carrots and sun-dried tomatoes. Sauté until the vegetables are tender.

Toss the pasta, sautéed vegetables, olives, 1/4 cup cheese, the garlic and salt in a serving bowl. Sprinkle with 1/4 cup cheese and let stand until the cheese melts. Serve with additional cheese, if desired. You may prepare in advance and reheat in the microwave just before serving.

Yield: 6 servings

HOT CURRIED FRUIT

1 (15-ounce) can peaches, drained and
   cut into 1-inch pieces

1 (15-ounce) can pears, drained and
   cut into 1-inch pieces

1 (20-ounce) can pineapple chunks, drained
   and cut into 1-inch pieces

2 or 3 bananas, cut into 1-inch pieces

1/2 cup dried cranberries, raisins or
   dried cherries

3/4 cup packed brown sugar

1/2 cup (1 stick) butter, melted

2 teaspoons curry powder

Preheat the oven to 300 degrees. Arrange the peaches, pears, pineapple and bananas in a shallow 2-quart baking dish and sprinkle with the cranberries. Mix the brown sugar, butter and curry powder in a bowl and spoon over the fruit mixture. Bake for 1 hour. Serve immediately.

Substitute different fruits to your liking or use chunky fruit cocktail. Sprinkle the top with 1/2 cup chopped or sliced nuts before baking, if desired.

Yield: 6 to 8 servings

SHERRIED HOT FRUIT

1 (15-ounce) can pear halves, drained

1 (17-ounce) can apricot halves, drained

1 (20-ounce) can pineapple chunks, drained

1 (16-ounce) can peach halves, drained

1/2 cup packed brown sugar

1/4 cup cooking sherry

1 (21-ounce) can cherry pie filling

1/4 cup (1/2 stick) butter, melted

Drain the pears, apricots, pineapple and peaches in one or two colanders over a bowl or bowls in the refrigerator for several hours.

Preheat the oven to 400 degrees. Layer the fruit in a large baking dish. Mix the brown sugar and sherry in a bowl until blended and pour over the prepared layers. Spread with the pie filling and drizzle with the butter. Bake for 45 minutes or until almost dry. Serve as a side dish or as a dessert topped with ice cream.

Yield: 10 to 12 servings

SPANISH STEWED GARBANZOS

1/2 cup water

1 teaspoon saffron threads

3 tablespoons extra-virgin olive oil

1 (14 ounce) can Italian plum tomatoes

13 ounces fresh spinach, chopped

1/2 cup flat-leaf parsley, chopped

3 garlic cloves, minced

1 teaspoon lemon juice

1 teaspoon honey

1 teaspoon ground cumin

1 teaspoon thyme

1 teaspoon salt

1/4 teaspoon freshly ground pepper

2 (15-ounce) cans garbanzos,
    drained and rinsed

Hot cooked couscous

Mix the water and saffron in a small saucepan. Bring to a simmer and remove from the heat. Let steep, covered, for 15 minutes. Heat the olive oil in a saucepan over medium heat for 1 minute. Stir in the tomatoes, spinach, parsley, garlic, lemon juice, honey, cumin, thyme, salt and pepper.

Cook for 3 minutes or until the spinach wilts, stirring constantly. Stir in the garbanzos and cook for about 2 minutes, stirring frequently. Stir in the saffron mixture and simmer for 3 to 5 minutes. Serve over hot cooked couscous.

Yield: 4 servings

FRENCHY'S FRENCH BEANS

CHEF JEAN-JACQUES BARILLEAU

2 pounds fresh green beans

Salt to taste

1 tablespoon butter

2 sweet onions, chopped

1 pint cherry tomatoes, cut into halves

2 tablespoons extra-virgin olive oil

Pepper to taste

Leaves of 4 sprigs of thyme

1 cup heavy whipping cream

Cook the green beans in boiling salted water in a saucepan for 3 to 5 minutes or until bright green and crisp. Drain and place in a serving dish. Melt the butter in a small saucepan and stir in the onions. Sauté until the onions are tender. Stir in the tomatoes. Cook, covered, for 2 minutes. Stir in the olive oil and season with salt and pepper. Add the thyme and cook, covered, for 2 minutes. Stir in the cream and cook just until heated through; do not boil. Drizzle over the green beans.

Yield: 6 servings

BALSAMIC-ROASTED CARROTS

2 pounds carrots

2 tablespoons olive oil

1/4 teaspoon salt

2 tablespoons balsamic vinegar

Preheat the oven to 425 degrees. Cut the carrots into $1/2 \times 3^1/2$-inch sticks. Toss the carrots with the olive oil and salt in a shallow roasting pan. Spread in a single layer and place the pan on the middle oven rack. Roast for 30 minutes or until golden brown and tender, stirring occasionally. Drizzle with the vinegar and shake the pan several times to distribute the vinegar. Roast for about 2 minutes or until most of the vinegar evaporates.

Nutrients Per Serving: Cal 163; Prot 2 g; Carbo 24 g; T Fat 7 g; Sat Fat 1 g; Chol 0 mg; Fiber 6 g; Sod 303 mg

Yield: 4 servings

Consider these common wine aromas when searching for that perfect complement to your meal:
- Caramelized—butter, butterscotch, chocolate, honey, molasses, soy sauce
- Earthy—mushroom, soil
- Floral—geranium, orange blossom, rose, violet
- Fruity—apple, apricot, banana, blackberry, black currant, cherry, fig, grapefruit, lemon, melon, peach, pineapple, raspberry, strawberry, strawberry jam
- Microbiological—sauerkraut, yeast
- Nutty—almond, hazelnut, walnut
- Pungent—alcohol, menthol
- Spicy— anise, black pepper or white pepper, cloves, licorice
- Vegetal—artichoke, asparagus, black olive, eucalyptus, green olive, mint, stemmy, cut grass, straw, tobacco
- Woody—cedar, coffee, oak, smoky

ROASTED CORN NIBLETS IN LIME BUTTER

8 ears of corn, shucked
1/4 cup olive oil
3 tablespoons butter

Juice of 2 limes
Salt and pepper to taste

Combine the corn with enough water to generously cover in a stockpot. Bring to a boil and remove from the heat. Let stand, covered, for 20 minutes and drain.

Preheat a charcoal grill. Brush the corn with the olive oil and arrange on the grill rack. Grill the until grill marks appear and the corn has had time to absorb some of the smoky flavor of the charcoal, rotating frequently. Melt the butter in a 2-quart saucepan and stir in the lime juice, salt and pepper. Toss the corn in the butter mixture and serve immediately.

Note: Charcoal grills bring optimal results, but to achieve a smoky flavor off the grill, use a well-seasoned cast iron skillet over direct heat.

Yield: 8 servings

CORN SOUFFLÉ

3 tablespoons butter or margarine
1 cup chopped onion
1 (9-ounce) package corn muffin mix
1 (17-ounce) can cream-style corn

1 cup sour cream
1/2 cup milk
2 eggs, beaten
1 cup (4 ounces) shredded cheese

Preheat the oven to 375 degrees. Melt the butter in a skillet and stir in the onion. Sauté until tender. Combine the corn muffin mix, corn, sour cream, milk and eggs in a bowl and mix well. Stir in the onion and 3/4 cup of the cheese.

Spoon into a greased baking dish and sprinkle with the remaining 1/4 cup cheese. Bake for 45 to 55 minutes or until light brown and puffed. Cover during the last 15 minutes of the baking process, if needed, to prevent overbrowning. You may freeze before baking. Thaw in the refrigerator and bake as directed above.

Yield: 8 servings

GRANDMOTHER'S EGGPLANT

2 eggplant, peeled, sliced and chopped

Salt to taste

1 large onion, chopped

2 fresh tomatoes, chopped (do not substitute)

1/4 cup (1/2 stick) butter, softened

Pepper to taste

1 egg

6 to 7 tablespoons butter

3/4 cup fresh bread crumbs

Cook the eggplant in boiling salted water in a saucepan for 10 to 15 minutes or until tender; drain. Combine the eggplant, onion, tomatoes, 1/4 cup butter, salt and pepper in a bowl and mix well. Stir in the egg and spoon into a buttered 11/2-quart baking dish.

Preheat the oven to 325 degrees. Melt 6 to 7 tablespoons butter in a small skillet. Add the bread crumbs and sauté just until bubbly. Spoon the bread crumbs over the prepared layer. Bake for 35 to 40 minutes or until brown. You may prepare in advance and store, covered, in the refrigerator. Sprinkle with the bread crumbs just before baking.

Yield: 6 servings

RATATOUILLE

Pronounced "ra-ta-too-ee," this classic Mediterranean dish can be served over angel hair pasta and accompanied by a crusty baguette to soak up the delicious juices.

1 eggplant, stem removed

Salt to taste

1/3 cup olive oil

1 large red bell pepper, coarsely chopped

4 tomatoes, peeled and coarsely chopped

2 onions, chopped

3 small zucchini, thinly sliced

2 small garlic cloves, crushed

2 teaspoons minced parsley

11/2 teaspoons salt

1 teaspoon sugar

1/4 teaspoon pepper

Cut the eggplant into 1/2-inch slices and cut into cubes. Combine the eggplant and salt to taste with enough water to cover in a bowl and let stand for 15 minutes; drain. Heat the olive oil in a skillet until sizzling and add the eggplant, bell pepper, tomatoes, onions and zucchini.

Cook, covered, for 5 minutes, stirring occasionally. Stir in the garlic and parsley and cook for 5 minutes. Mix in 11/2 teaspoons salt, the sugar and pepper and cook, covered, for 5 to 10 minutes longer to allow the flavors to blend, stirring occasionally. Serve hot.

Nutrients Per Serving: Cal 182; Prot 3 g; Carbo 17 g; T Fat 13 g; Sat Fat 2 g; Chol 0 mg; Fiber 6 g; Sod 596 mg

Yield: 6 servings

DOWNTOWN FARMERS' MARKET

Patronizing Sarasota's local farmers' market is a treasured weekly ritual that makes everyone want to get up early on Saturday morning and head for downtown. It's the place to meet and greet, have breakfast with friends, and then to browse cheerful stalls for fresh flowers, delectable fresh fruits, vegetables, herbs, and more. It's the place to chat with growers, trade recipes, and learn about heirloom produce. We hear a lot these days about sustainable living; the Farmers' Market is where it begins for many local cooks (and fortunate eaters) in this lucky city.

VIDALIA ONION CLASSIC CASSEROLE

1/2 cup (1 stick) butter

4 large Vidalia onions or any sweet onions,
   cut into 1/2-inch slices

2/3 cup chicken broth

1/3 cup dry sherry

2 tablespoons all-purpose flour

1 1/2 cups soft bread crumbs

1/2 cup (2 ounces) shredded sharp
   Cheddar cheese

2 tablespoons grated Parmesan cheese

Preheat the oven to 350 degrees. Melt the butter in a large skillet and add the onions. Sauté until tender. Stir in the broth, sherry and flour and cook until slightly thickened, stirring constantly. Spoon into a baking dish and sprinkle with the bread crumbs, Cheddar cheese and Parmesan cheese. Bake for 20 to 30 minutes or until light brown and bubbly. You may prepare in advance and store, covered, in the refrigerator. Bake just before serving.

Yield: 6 servings

ROASTED ROSEMARY NEW POTATOES

Serve this versatile side dish with a wide range of entrées—succulent pork roast or beef tenderloin, roasted chicken or fish—even with a dinner omelet.

2 pounds new potatoes

1 onion, sliced

2 tablespoons olive oil

1 teaspoon kosher salt

1 teaspoon pepper

Leaves of 3 to 5 sprigs of rosemary

Preheat the oven to 400 degrees. Cut the potatoes into halves or quarters depending on size. Toss the potatoes and onion with the olive oil, salt, pepper and rosemary in a bowl until coated. Arrange in a single layer on a baking sheet and roast for 45 minutes or until light brown and tender, stirring two or three times.

Nutrients Per Serving: Cal 66; Prot 2 g; Carbo 7 g; T Fat 3 g; Sat Fat ,1 g; Chol 0 mg; Fiber 3 g; Sod 243 mg

Yield: 8 servings

SPINACH WITH PINE NUTS

This elegant dish is so easy and adaptable: Substitute slivered almonds and Worcestershire sauce for the pine nuts and balsamic, or add crumbled gorgonzola cheese just before serving.

1 shallot, finely chopped
2 garlic cloves, minced
3 tablespoons olive oil
1/4 cup pine nuts
10 ounces fresh spinach
Dash of salt
Dash of pepper
3 to 4 tablespoons balsamic vinegar

Sauté the shallot and garlic in the olive oil in a large nonstick skillet over medium heat just until the shallot is tender. Stir in the pine nuts and cook until the pine nuts begin to brown. Add the spinach and cook just until the spinach wilts, stirring frequently. Stir in the salt and pepper. Add the vinegar and toss gently to coat. Serve immediately.

Nutrients Per Serving: Cal 189; Prot 3 g; Carbo 10 g; T Fat 16 g; Sat Fat 2 g; Chol 0 mg; Fiber 2 g; Sod 133 mg

Yield: 4 servings

Working with Onions and Garlic
- To cut an onion without crying . . . cut the onion in half and run the flat side under warm water for 5 seconds. Then place the flat side face down on the cutting board and slice as desired.
- To eliminate the odor of onions and garlic on your skin after handling, rub your hands against stainless steel under running water.

SPINACH- AND RICOTTA-STUFFED ZUCCHINI

4 zucchini

2 teaspoons olive oil

1 onion, chopped

4 garlic cloves, minced

1 (10-ounce) package frozen chopped
   spinach, thawed, drained and squeezed

1/4 teaspoon pepper

1/8 teaspoon ground nutmeg

1 cup part-skim ricotta cheese

1/4 cup (1 ounce) grated Parmesan cheese

1 egg, beaten

2 tablespoons raisins

1 tablespoon chopped walnuts

Cut the zucchini lengthwise into halves. Scoop out the pulp, leaving a 1/4-inch-thick shell; discard the pulp. Place the shells in a saucepan and cover with boiling water. Cook for 4 minutes and drain. Rinse with cold water. Arrange in a single layer on a baking sheet.

Preheat the oven to 350 degrees. Heat the olive oil in a skillet over medium heat for 1 minute. Add the onion and garlic and cook for 5 minutes, stirring frequently. Stir in the spinach, pepper and nutmeg and cook, covered, for 2 minutes; remove the cover. Cook for 2 minutes longer or until the liquid evaporates. Remove from the heat and let stand until cool. Stir in the remaining ingredients. Spoon into the zucchini shells and bake for 20 minutes.

Nutrients Per Serving: Cal 120; Prot 8 g; Carbo 10 g; T Fat 6 g; Sat Fat 3 g; Chol 38 mg; Fiber 3 g; Sod 123 mg
Nutritional profile includes the whole zucchini.

Yield: 8 servings

94

SWEET POTATO BAKE

6 large sweet potatoes, peeled

6 ripe pears, peeled and each cut into
   8 wedges

3/4 cup packed brown sugar

1/2 cup orange juice

1/3 cup pear brandy

1/4 cup (1/2 stick) butter

1/2 cup golden raisins

Cut the sweet potatoes into 1/2-inch slices. Combine with enough water to cover in a saucepan and bring to a boil. Reduce the heat to low and simmer for 12 to 15 minutes or just until the sweet potatoes are tender; drain.

Preheat the oven to 375 degrees. Layer the sweet potatoes and pears alternately in a baking dish. Combine the brown sugar, orange juice, brandy, butter and raisins in a small saucepan and cook over medium heat until the brown sugar dissolves and the butter melts, stirring frequently. Pour over the prepared layers and bake for 30 minutes or until light brown and bubbly. Serve immediately.

Yield: 10 to 12 servings

BAKED BLUE CHEESE TOMATOES

2 ripe medium to large tomatoes
Kosher salt and pepper to taste
2 teaspoons chopped fresh basil
1/2 cup (8 tablespoons) crumbled blue cheese
1/4 cup bread crumbs

Preheat the oven to 350 degrees. Cut the tomatoes horizontally into halves. Arrange cut side up in a baking pan. Season with salt and pepper. Sprinkle each tomato half with 1/2 teaspoon of the basil, 2 tablespoons of the cheese and 1 tablespoon of the bread crumbs. Bake for 12 to 15 minutes or until light brown and heated through.

Nutrients Per Serving: Cal 100; Prot 5 g; Carbo 8 g; T Fat 5 g; Sat Fat 3 g; Chol 13 mg; Fiber 1 g; Sod 289 mg

Yield: 4 servings

TEMPTING TOMATO PIE

4 tomatoes, sliced
1 unbaked (9-inch) deep-dish pie shell
8 to 10 basil leaves, chopped
1/3 cup chopped green onions
Salt and pepper to taste
1 cup *Publix* mayonnaise
1 cup (4 ounces) shredded mozzarella cheese
1 cup (4 ounces) shredded Cheddar cheese

Preheat the oven to 350 degrees. Arrange the tomatoes in the pie shell and sprinkle with the basil, green onions, salt and pepper. Mix the mayonnaise, mozzarella cheese and Cheddar cheese in a bowl and spread over the prepared layers. Bake for 30 minutes or until the cheese melts and the topping begins to brown.

Yield: 6 servings

Apricot-Glazed Pork Tenderloin and Asparagus, page 113

Simply
Satisfying

SIESTA GRILLED CHICKEN

4 (5-ounce) boneless skinless chicken breasts
1/2 cup chopped fresh cilantro
1/4 cup olive oil
Juice of 2 limes
2 tablespoons chopped bottled jalapeño chiles
2 garlic cloves, minced
1 teaspoon salt
1 teaspoon black pepper

Arrange the chicken in a shallow dish. Mix the cilantro, olive oil, lime juice, jalapeño chiles and garlic in a bowl and pour over the chicken, turning to coat. Sprinkle with the salt and pepper. Marinate, covered, in the refrigerator for 8 to 10 hours, turning occasionally.

Preheat the grill. Arrange the chicken on the grill rack. Grill for 20 minutes or until cooked through, turning halfway through the grilling process.

Note: Perfect when accompanied with fresh guacamole and pico de gallo.

Nutrients Per Serving: Cal 279; Prot 29 g; Carbo 2 g; T Fat 17 g; Sat Fat 3 g; Chol 78 mg; Fiber <1 g; Sod 722 mg
The nutritional profile includes all of the marinade.

Yield: 4 servings

GRILLED CHICKEN WITH SWEET CHILI GLAZE

4 (5-ounce) chicken breasts
Salt and pepper to taste
1/4 cup honey
1 tablespoon chili powder

Preheat the grill. Season the chicken generously with salt and pepper and arrange the chicken on the grill rack. Grill until cooked through, turning once or twice. Mix the honey and chili powder in a bowl. Drizzle each chicken breast with one-fourth of the glaze and serve immediately.

Nutrients Per Serving: Cal 225; Prot 29 g; Carbo 19 g; T Fat 4 g; Sat Fat 1 g; Chol 78 mg; Fiber <1 g; Sod 113 mg

Yield: 4 servings

Sarasota's beautiful weather and proximity to beaches blanketed with sparkling white sands make outdoor grilling a favorite pastime. When using a gas grill, remember that the propane will run out either while you are heating up the grill or while you are cooking! Make sure you always have an extra full propane tank on hand and you will never have to worry about your grill running out of fuel while you are cooking.

CHICKEN BREASTS WITH APPLE STUFFING

1/3 pound bulk hot Italian sausage

2 ribs celery, chopped

1/2 cup minced onion

1/4 green bell pepper, chopped

1/4 red bell pepper, chopped

Minced fresh garlic to taste

1 apple, peeled and chopped

1 slice whole wheat bread, torn into 1/2-inch pieces

2 tablespoons chopped fresh parsley

1 teaspoon thyme

1 egg, lightly beaten, or equivalent amount of egg substitute

1 teaspoon grated orange zest

6 (5-ounce) boneless skinless chicken breasts

3 tablespoons butter

1/2 cup orange juice

Cook the sausage in a large nonstick skillet over medium-high heat for 5 minutes, stirring until crumbly; drain. Stir in the celery, onion, bell peppers and garlic and cook over medium heat for 10 minutes, stirring occasionally. Mix the apple, bread, parsley and thyme in a bowl and stir in the sausage mixture, egg and orange zest.

Preheat the oven to 400 degrees. Pound the chicken breasts between sheets of waxed paper with a meat mallet until flattened. Spread 3 tablespoons of the sausage mixture in the center of each chicken breast and roll to enclose the filling. Secure with wooden picks.

Melt the butter in a 12-inch skillet over high heat. Sear the rolls in the hot butter on all sides for about 4 minutes. Arrange the chicken rolls seam side down in a lightly greased 9×13-inch baking dish, reserving the skillet drippings. Bake the chicken rolls for 10 to 12 minutes or until cooked through.

Add the orange juice to the reserved drippings and bring to a boil, scraping the bottom of the skillet with a wooden spoon to dislodge any brown bits. Discard the wooden picks from the rolls and drizzle with the orange juice mixture.

Yield: 6 servings

STUFFED CHICKEN BREASTS

4 (5-ounce) boneless skinless chicken breasts

2/3 cup crumbled goat cheese

3 tablespoons sliced sun-dried tomatoes

1 tablespoon chopped fresh basil

Salt and pepper to taste

1 cup bread crumbs

1 tablespoon butter, melted

Preheat the oven to 375 degrees. Make a pocket in the side of each chicken breast. Mix the cheese, sun-dried tomatoes and basil in a bowl and stuff each pocket evenly with the cheese mixture. Secure with wooden picks. Sprinkle with salt and pepper.

Toss the bread crumbs with the butter in a bowl until coated. Press over the surface of the chicken breasts and arrange in a single layer in a greased baking pan. Bake for 25 to 30 minutes or until cooked through.

Nutrients Per Serving: Cal 359; Prot 37 g; Carbo 21 g; T Fat 13 g; Sat Fat 7 g; Chol 101 mg; Fiber 2 g; Sod 436 mg

Yield: 4 servings

MEXICAN CHICKEN

The perfect spicy complement to our cool and refreshing Smashing Sangria (page 34). Let the fiesta begin!

8 (5-ounce) boneless skinless chicken breasts

1 (7-ounce) can diced green chiles

4 ounces Monterey Jack cheese, cut into 8 strips

1/2 cup dry bread crumbs

1/4 cup (1 ounce) grated Parmesan cheese

1 tablespoon chili powder

1/4 teaspoon ground cumin

Salt and pepper to taste

6 tablespoons butter, melted

Preheat the oven to 400 degrees. Pound the chicken breasts between sheets of waxed paper with a meat mallet until flattened. Place equal portions of the green chiles and one strip of the Monterey Jack cheese on each chicken breast and roll to enclose. Secure with wooden picks.

Mix the bread crumbs, Parmesan cheese, chili powder, cumin, salt and pepper in a shallow dish. Dip the chicken rolls in the butter and coat with the bread crumb mixture. Place the rolls seam side down in a baking dish and drizzle with the remaining butter. Bake for 20 minutes.

Yield: 8 servings

MOROCCAN CHICKEN

1 tablespoon olive oil	1 teaspoon ground cinnamon
4 (5-ounce) chicken breasts	1 teaspoon curry powder
1 onion, chopped	1 teaspoon ground cumin
6 garlic cloves, chopped	1 teaspoon crushed red pepper
2 (14-ounce) cans stewed tomatoes	1 teaspoon salt
1 cup dried apricots	4 or 5 red potatoes, coarsely chopped
2 tablespoons lemon juice	1 cup baby carrots

Heat the olive oil in a Dutch oven and add the chicken. Cook for 3 minutes or until brown on all sides, turning frequently. Remove the chicken to a platter, reserving the pan drippings.

Preheat the oven to 375 degrees. Cook the onion and garlic in the reserved pan drippings for several minutes, stirring occasionally. Stir in the tomatoes, apricots, lemon juice, cinnamon, curry powder, cumin, red pepper and salt. Return the chicken to the Dutch oven and bake, covered, for 1 1/2 to 2 hours, adding the potatoes and carrots 30 minutes before the end of the baking process.

Note: This intense, spice-laced stew calls for a robust, powerful wine. Try a Rioja from Spain, a gutsy California cabernet sauvignon, or a Rhône wine from France. Anything less would shrink meekly in the presence of the red pepper, cumin, curry and cinnamon in the dish. Any good Chateauneuf du Pape would be a good French choice. Another possibility is a big, fruity red zinfandel.

Nutrients Per Serving: Cal 426; Prot 36 g; Carbo 52 g; T Fat 7 g; Sat Fat 1 g; Chol 78 mg; Fiber 11 g; Sod 1111 mg

Yield: 4 servings

COMPANY CHICKEN

8 (5-ounce) boneless skinless chicken breasts	1/2 cup white wine
8 slices Swiss cheese	2 cups crushed herb-seasoned stuffing mix
1 (10-ounce) can cream of chicken soup	1/2 cup (1 stick) butter, melted

Preheat the oven to 350 degrees. Arrange the chicken in a single layer in a shallow baking pan. Top each chicken breast with one slice of the cheese. Mix the soup and wine in a bowl and pour over the chicken. Sprinkle with the stuffing mix and drizzle with the butter. Bake for 40 to 45 minutes or until the chicken is cooked through.

Yield: 8 servings

FRED'S CHICKEN POTPIE

CHEF MARIO MARTINEZ, FRED'S

Mushroom Mirepoix

2 tablespoons butter, chopped

1 cup chopped onion

1 cup chopped celery

1 cup chopped carrots

1 tablespoon minced garlic

1 bay leaf

1 1/2 teaspoons dried thyme leaves

2 cups sliced mushrooms

1 1/2 teaspoons kosher salt

1 teaspoon ground white pepper

1 tablespoon thinly sliced chives

Potpie

1/4 cup (1/2 stick) butter

1/2 cup all-purpose flour

2 cups milk

1 cup heavy cream

1 tablespoon chicken base

2 tablespoons medium-dry sherry

3 cups coarsely chopped cooked chicken

1 cup frozen green peas, thawed

2 sheets frozen short-crust pie pastry, thawed

1 egg yolk

1 tablespoon water

For the mirepoix, melt the butter in a heavy skillet over high heat until hot but not smoking. Stir in the onion, celery, carrots, garlic and bay leaf and sauté for 3 to 5 minutes. Add the thyme, mushrooms, salt and white pepper and sauté for 5 to 7 minutes longer. Discard the bay leaf. Spread the mushroom mixture on a baking sheet and let stand until room temperature. Mix with the chives in a bowl and chill, covered, until needed.

For the potpie, preheat the oven to 400 degrees. Melt the butter in a large saucepan over medium-high heat. Add the flour and stir until blended. Stir in the milk, cream, chicken base and sherry and cook until thickened, stirring constantly. Mix in the chicken and simmer, covered, for 5 to 7 minutes, stirring occasionally. Let stand until room temperature and stir in the peas and mirepoix. Spoon into six 1 1/2-cup ramekins. Rub additional butter or vegetable oil on the rims of the ramekins and arrange the ramekins on a baking sheet.

Cut six rounds out of the pie pastry large enough to cover the tops of the ramekins and drape slightly over the edges. Arrange the rounds over the tops of the ramekins and cut a small hole in the center of each. Brush the dough with a mixture of the egg yolk and water and bake for 20 to 30 minutes or until brown and bubbly. Serve the ramekins on serving plates lined with a pot holder or folded napkin.

Yield: 6 servings

CREAMY CHICKEN BAKE

6 (5-ounce) chicken breasts
6 slices bacon
1 cup sour cream
1 (10-ounce) can cream of chicken or cream of mushroom soup
1/4 cup sherry or white wine
1/4 teaspoon pepper
1 1/2 teaspoons chopped fresh parsley
Hot cooked rice or noodles

Preheat the oven to 350 degrees. Trim the chicken breasts of excess fat and wrap each with one slice of the bacon. Arrange the chicken breasts in a single layer in a baking dish. Mix the soup, sherry and pepper in a bowl and spread over the chicken. Bake for 1 1/2 hours and sprinkle with the parsley. Serve over hot cooked rice or noodles. You may freeze for future use.

Yield: 6 servings

General Rules for Pairing Wine with Food
- The heavier the dish, the heavier the wine.
- Select light-bodied wines to pair with lighter food and fuller-bodied wines to go with heartier, more flavorful dishes. Serve red with meat and white with fish or fowl.
- Sweet sauces and glazes like tomato sauce, teriyaki, and honey mustard react well with slightly sweet wines such as chenin blanc, white zinfandel, and riesling.
- Highly acidic foods like balsamic vinaigrette dressing, soy sauce, or fish with a squeeze of lemon pair well with wines higher in acid including sauvignon blanc, pinot grigio, pinot noir, and even white zinfandel.
- Bitter foods like bitter greens, kalamata olives, and charbroiled meats are complemented by fruity wines such as chardonnay, cabernet sauvignon, and merlot.

Chicken and Vegetable Skillet

1 envelope onion soup mix or mushroom and onion soup mix
1/4 cup water
2 tablespoons olive oil
1 tablespoon fresh lime juice or lemon juice
1 teaspoon Italian seasoning
1/2 teaspoon garlic powder
1/8 teaspoon cayenne pepper
1 pound boneless skinless chicken breasts, cut into strips
1 (16-ounce) package *Publix* frozen mixed vegetables

Combine the soup mix, water, olive oil, lime juice, Italian seasoning, garlic powder and cayenne pepper in a large skillet and mix well. Let stand for 5 minutes. Bring to a boil and stir in the chicken and mixed vegetables.

Cook for 8 to 10 minutes or until the chicken is cooked through, stirring occasionally. Serve with a salad and your favorite bread.

Nutrients Per Serving: Cal 259; Prot 27 g; Carbo 17 g; T Fat 10 g; Sat Fat 2 g; Chol 63 mg; Fiber 5 g; Sod 261 mg

Yield: 4 servings

CHICKEN FRANÇAIS

Chicken

2 eggs

1 tablespoon sugar

1 tablespoon grated Parmesan cheese

4 (5-ounce) chicken breasts

1 cup all-purpose flour

Olive oil for frying

Lemon Sherry Sauce

1/4 cup (1/2 stick) butter

1/4 cup dry sherry

1/4 cup lemon juice

2 tablespoons garlic powder

2 chicken bouillon cubes, or 1 cup chicken broth

For the chicken, whisk the eggs, sugar and cheese in a bowl. Coat the chicken breasts with the flour and dip in the egg mixture. Heat olive oil in a large skillet over medium heat. Fry the chicken in the hot oil until golden brown on all sides; drain.

For the sauce, melt the butter in a saucepan over low heat. Stir in the sherry, lemon juice, garlic powder and bouillon cubes and simmer, covered, for 20 minutes, stirring occasionally. Add the chicken and simmer for 10 minutes longer. Remove the chicken to a platter and drizzle with any remaining sauce.

Yield: 4 servings

CHICKEN PICCATA

2 boneless skinless chicken breasts
3 eggs
1 tablespoon milk
1 cup all-purpose flour
1/2 cup (1 stick) unsalted butter, clarified
1 garlic clove, crushed
Salt and pepper to taste
1 tablespoon lemon juice, or to taste
1 cup white wine
1 tablespoon rinsed drained capers

Pound the chicken 1/4 inch thick between sheets of waxed paper. Cut each chicken breast into three or four pieces. Whisk the eggs and milk in a shallow dish until blended. Coat the chicken lightly with the flour and dip in the egg mixture.

Heat the clarified butter and garlic in a large sauté pan until the butter is hot but not smoking. Add the chicken to the hot butter mixture and sprinkle lightly with salt and pepper, moving the pan constantly to keep the chicken from sticking. Cook for 4 to 5 minutes. Pour in the lemon juice and move the pan in a back and forward motion. Add the wine and cook for 2 minutes, continuing to move the pan in a back and forth motion. Add the capers and cook for 2 minutes longer or until the sauce is thickened. Serve immediately. You may substitute veal or grouper for the chicken.

Yield: 4 servings

TURKEY STROGANOFF

2 tablespoons vegetable oil

1 pound ground turkey

1 onion, chopped

1/2 cup white wine or chicken broth

2 cups mushrooms, sliced

1/2 teaspoon ground nutmeg

Salt and pepper to taste

1 cup cottage cheese

1/2 cup plain low-fat yogurt

1 tablespoon lemon juice

8 ounces fettuccini, cooked and drained

Paprika to taste

Heat the oil in a large skillet and add the turkey and onion. Cook until the ground turkey is light brown and crumbly and the onion is tender, stirring constantly; drain. Stir in the wine and mushrooms and bring to a simmer. Season with the nutmeg, salt and pepper. Stir in the cottage cheese, yogurt and lemon juice.

Cook until heated through and of the desired consistency, stirring occasionally. Spoon the turkey mixture over the hot cooked pasta on a serving platter. Sprinkle with paprika.

Yield: 4 servings

Try using a little Mojo seasoning (Cuban garlic/citrus sauce) in your favorite chicken, pork, or fish marinade. A tablespoon or two should be enough for a subtle change in the flavor of your dish.

Swiss, Turkey and Ham Bake

2 tablespoons butter or Smart Balance

1/2 cup chopped onion

3 tablespoons all-purpose flour

1/2 teaspoon salt

1/4 teaspoon pepper

1 (3-ounce) can sliced mushrooms

1 cup light cream

1/4 cup dry sherry

2 cups (1/2-inch) cubes cooked turkey

2 cups (1/2-inch) cubes cooked ham

1 (5-ounce) can sliced water chestnuts, drained

1 cup (4 ounces) shredded Swiss cheese

1/2 cup (2 ounces) shredded sharp white Cheddar cheese
  (optional)

1 1/2 cups soft bread crumbs

3 tablespoons butter, melted

Preheat the oven to 400 degrees. Melt 2 tablespoons butter in a skillet and add the onion. Cook until the onion is tender but not brown. Blend in the flour, salt and pepper. Stir in the mushrooms, cream and sherry.

Cook until thickened, stirring frequently. Stir in the turkey, ham and water chestnuts. Spoon into a 1- or 2-quart baking dish and sprinkle with the Swiss cheese and Cheddar cheese. Toss the bread crumbs and 3 tablespoons butter in a bowl and sprinkle over the prepared layers. Bake for 25 minutes.

Yield: 6 servings

JOHN RINGLING CAUSEWAY, VAN WEZEL PERFORMING ARTS HALL, AND SARASOTA WATERFRONT

The new John Ringling Causeway offers a spectacular view of Sarasota Bay, whether you are making a day trip to St. Armand's Circle or returning to the mainland. When you enjoy food experiences at St. Armand's Circle, you're just naturally part of café society. This charming village of chic shops and diverse restaurants that once belonged to circus impresario John Ringling includes a wealth of places to dine casually outdoors under colorful umbrellas. You'll relax, nibble, and watch the parade of international visitors saunter by. Create your own moveable feast by ordering a cocktail at one café; then move on to dinner at another. For dessert, have an ice cream cone or piece of homemade fudge in hand while you stroll the circle window-shopping . . . or discover another sidewalk café, nestle in, and indulge in something more deliciously complex. As you drift back to the mainland after a day of indulgences, enjoy the view of the Sarasota waterfront, which includes the amethyst Van Wezel Performing Arts Hall. The Van Wezel has welcomed a broad range of performers and shows, including world-class symphonies, renowned dance companies, jazz artists, pop legends, and the best of Broadway.

HAM DI PARMA

1/3 cup butter

6 ounces fresh mushrooms, sliced

2 tablespoons grated onion

1/4 cup all-purpose flour

1/4 teaspoon oregano

1/8 teaspoon pepper

2 cups whipping cream

1 pound cooked ham, cut into strips

3/4 cup dry white wine, or liquid of choice

1/3 cup sliced green olives or pimento-stuffed olives

1 pimento, cut into strips

8 ounces spaghetti, cooked and drained

1/2 cup (2 ounces) shredded or grated Parmesan cheese

Melt the butter in a large skillet and add the mushrooms and onion. Cook for 5 minutes, stirring occasionally. Remove the mushroom mixture to a platter using a slotted spoon, reserving the pan drippings. Blend the flour, oregano and pepper into the reserved pan drippings. Add the cream gradually, stirring constantly. Bring to a boil and boil for 1 minute. Stir in the ham, wine, olives and pimento.

Preheat the broiler. Toss the pasta with 1/4 cup of the cheese in a bowl. Spread in a 2 1/2 quart baking dish or 10×15-inch baking pan with 2-inch sides. Spoon the ham mixture over the pasta and sprinkle with the remaining 1/4 cup cheese. Broil 4 to 6 inches from the heat source until light brown and heated through. You may freeze for future use.

Yield: 8 servings

APRICOT-GLAZED PORK TENDERLOIN AND ASPARAGUS

2 tablespoons olive oil

3 tablespoons finely chopped fresh rosemary

3 tablespoons minced garlic

1 teaspoon salt

1/2 teaspoon freshly ground pepper

2 pounds pork tenderloin

1 pound asparagus

1/2 cup apricot preserves

Preheat the oven to 400 degrees. Mix the olive oil, rosemary, garlic, salt and pepper in a bowl and spread over the surface of the tenderloin. Place the tenderloin in a baking pan and let stand at room temperature for 30 minutes. Snap off the thick woody ends of the asparagus spears and discard. Blanch the asparagus in boiling water in a saucepan for 2 minutes and drain.

Heat the preserves in a small saucepan over medium-low heat until melted and baste the tenderloin with the preserves. Roast until a meat thermometer registers 170 degrees, basting every 10 minutes with the preserves. Add the asparagus to the baking pan 10 minutes before end of the roasting process and pour the remaining preserves over the asparagus and tenderloin. Roast for 10 minutes longer. Let stand for 10 minutes before slicing.

Nutrients Per Serving: Cal 310; Prot 33 g; Carbo 23 g; T Fat 10 g; Sat Fat 2 g; Chol 84 mg; Fiber 2 g; Sod 461 mg

Yield: 6 servings   *Photograph for this recipe appears on page 96.*

113

Serve Jezebel Sauce as an accompaniment with ham or pork, or drizzle over cream cheese and serve with crackers for an appetizer. To make Jezebel Sauce, heat one 18-ounce jar apple jelly in a saucepan until melted and cool slightly. Stir in one 18-ounce jar pineapple preserves, 1/2 small jar prepared horseradish, 1/2 small can dry mustard, and 2 teaspoons pepper.

HERBED PORK ROAST

2½ teaspoons salt

1 teaspoon pepper

1 teaspoon crushed thyme

½ teaspoon ground nutmeg

1 (4- to 6-pound) pork loin

1 (10-ounce) can chicken broth

2 carrots, cut into small chunks

2 onions, chopped

2 large garlic cloves, chopped

4 whole cloves

3 bay leaves

Sprigs of parsley to taste

Chopped celery leaves to taste

Preheat the oven to 450 degrees. Mix the salt, pepper, thyme and nutmeg in a bowl and rub over the surface of the pork. Arrange the pork in a roasting pan and roast for 30 minutes. Reduce the oven temperature to 350 degrees and add the broth, carrots, onions, garlic, cloves, bay leaves, parsley and celery leaves to the roasting pan.

Roast, covered, for 3 hours or until the pork is the desired degree of doneness, basting frequently with the pan drippings. Remove the pork to a platter and skim the fat from the pan drippings. Discard the cloves and bay leaves and pour the pan drippings and vegetables into a blender. Process until smooth and serve with the pork.

Serve with Barley and Mushroom Casserole (page 84). You may prepare one day in advance and store, covered, in the refrigerator. Reheat before serving.

Nutrients Per Serving: Cal 414; Prot 55 g; Carbo 4 g; T Fat 18 g; Sat Fat 7 g; Chol 154 mg; Fiber 1 g; Sod 841 mg

Yield: 10 servings

Hirinó me Fassólia

2½ pounds boneless pork loin, 1 inch thick
1 onion, finely chopped
1 (20-ounce) package frozen Italian green beans
2 cups coarsely chopped celery
1 teaspoon oregano
½ teaspoon Worcestershire sauce
Salt and pepper to taste
1 (16-ounce) can diced tomatoes
1 (8-ounce) can tomato sauce
2 garlic cloves, minced (optional)

Brown the pork on all sides in a Dutch oven. Remove the pork to a platter using a slotted spoon, reserving the pan drippings. Sauté the onion in the reserved pan drippings until tender. Remove the onion to a bowl using a slotted spoon, discarding the pan drippings. Combine the green beans, celery and a small amount of water in a microwave-safe dish and microwave on High for 6 minutes; drain.

Layer the pork, onion, oregano, Worcestershire sauce, salt, pepper, tomatoes, tomato sauce and green bean mixture in the Dutch oven. Simmer over low heat for 1 hour. For variety, add mushrooms. You may freeze for future use.

Nutrients Per Serving: Cal 351; Prot 41 g; Carbo 18 g; T Fat 13 g; Sat Fat 5 g; Chol 107 mg; Fiber 6 g; Sod 411 mg

Yield: 6 servings

When entertaining, it is best to serve dishes you're familiar with and have cooked before. But if you try something new, be sure to practice beforehand and get the seasonings just right. Don't surprise your guests with a complex creation that doesn't work out!

Simply Satisfying

SHREDDED PORK

Pork

1/3 cup packed brown sugar

1 teaspoon paprika

1 teaspoon salt

1/2 teaspoon pepper

1/2 teaspoon garlic powder or garlic salt

1 (7- to 8-pound) Boston butt roast

Barbecue Vinaigrette Sauce

2/3 cup cider vinegar

4 teaspoons Worcestershire sauce

2 teaspoons salt

1 1/2 teaspoons sugar

1/2 teaspoon black pepper

1/2 teaspoon dry mustard

1 teaspoon red pepper flakes

1/2 teaspoon garlic salt

1/4 teaspoon cayenne pepper

For the pork, mix the brown sugar, paprika, salt, pepper and garlic powder in a bowl. Coat the pork with the brown sugar mixture and place in a slow cooker. Cook, covered, on Low for 8 to 10 hours. The flavor is enhanced if cooked closer to 10 hours.

For the sauce, combine the vinegar, Worcestershire sauce, salt, sugar, black pepper, dry mustard, red pepper flakes, garlic salt and cayenne pepper in a jar with a tight-fitting lid and shake to mix. The flavor of the sauce improves if prepared at least one day in advance.

Drain the pork and return to the slow cooker. Shred the pork with two forks and mix in the sauce. Serve the pork alone or on buns.

Yield: 10 to 12 servings

ITALIAN BEEF

Never underestimate the power of leftovers, especially this delicious beef. Make hot or cold sandwiches the next day.

2 teaspoons salt
2 teaspoons basil
2 teaspoons parsley flakes, or sprigs of fresh parsley
1 teaspoon black pepper
1 teaspoon crushed red pepper
1/2 teaspoon garlic powder
2 bay leaves, crushed
1 (5- to 7-pound) beef brisket
3 cups water

Preheat the oven to 350 degrees. Mix the salt, basil, parsley flakes, black pepper, red pepper, garlic powder and bay leaves in a bowl and rub the salt mixture over the surface of the brisket. Arrange the brisket in a baking pan and pour the water around the brisket.

Bake, covered, for 3 hours. Remove the brisket to a platter, reserving the pan drippings. Strain the pan drippings, discarding the solids. Slice the brisket as desired and drizzle the strained pan drippings over the brisket. Serve immediately with crusty French bread. You may substitute one sliced garlic clove for the garlic powder. Make slits in the brisket and insert the sliced garlic. Freeze for future use, if desired.

Yield: 10 servings

CONTEMPORARY BEEF WELLINGTON

Duxelles

1/4 cup (1/2 stick) butter

1 tablespoon finely chopped shallot

1 pound mushrooms, finely chopped

1/4 cup (or less) madeira

2 tablespoons minced parsley

Salt and pepper to taste

Ground nutmeg to taste

Beef Wellington

6 (8-ounce) beef fillets, at room temperature

Salt and pepper to taste

12 sheets phyllo pastry

1 cup (2 sticks) butter, melted

For the duxelles, melt the butter in a skillet and stir in the shallot. Cook over low heat until tender. Stir in the mushrooms and cook for 10 to 15 minutes over low heat or until all the liquid evaporates and the mixture is very dark in color, stirring occasionally. Stir in the wine, parsley, salt, pepper and nutmeg. Increase the heat slightly and cook until all the liquid evaporates. Chill, covered, in the refrigerator until needed.

For the Beef Wellington, preheat the oven to 375 degrees. Trim the fillets of all fat and season with salt and pepper. Cut two sheets of plastic wrap slightly longer than the phyllo and arrange the sheets overlapping on a work surface. Cover the phyllo with a damp paper towel.

Stack two sheets of the phyllo on the plastic wrap, brushing each sheet with some of the melted butter. Arrange one fillet 3 inches from the end of the narrow edge of the phyllo stack and spread the fillet with 1/4 cup of the duxelles. Fold 3 inches of the phyllo over the fillet and brush with melted butter. Using the plastic wrap, turn the fillet and phyllo over and brush the exposed phyllo with melted butter. Fold in the long sides of the phyllo and brush with melted butter. Continue folding the phyllo around the steak, brushing with melted butter after each turn.

Arrange seam side down on a buttered baking sheet. Repeat the process with the remaining phyllo, remaining butter and remaining fillets. Bake for 20 to 30 minutes or until the pastry is puffed and golden brown and the fillets register 140 degrees on a meat thermometer for rare. Freeze for future use, if desired.

Yield: 6 servings

STEAK TERIYAKI

1 (1½-pound) flank steak or skirt steak
1 (10- or 14-ounce) can beef broth
¼ cup soy sauce
2 tablespoons lemon juice
1 to 2 tablespoons brown sugar
1 garlic clove, minced

Score the steak against the grain. Mix the broth, soy sauce, lemon juice, brown sugar and garlic in a shallow dish and add the steak, turning to coat. Marinate, covered, in the refrigerator for 8 to 10 hours or for up to 3 days.

Preheat the grill. Grill the steak over hot coals to the desired degree of doneness, turning once or twice. Slice as desired.

Yield: 2 to 4 servings

When talking about beaujolais, the French have an expression, "A servir jeune, a boire frais." This translates roughly to "Serve me young, drink me chilled," an expression that succinctly explains why this refreshing red is perfect for picnics and barbeques. Bursting with grape aroma and fruity charm, the wine lends itself to a slight chill (about 45 minutes in the refrigerator), which enhances the wine's zesty character. Besides the warm-weather appeal of a chilled red wine, beaujolais has an acidity level that stands up to the variety of foods usually served at picnics and barbeques; it is just about the perfect red for casual food.

BODACIOUS BLUE CHEESE BURGERS

1 1/2 pounds lean ground chuck
1/2 cup bread crumbs
1/3 cup blue cheese salad dressing
1/2 envelope onion soup mix
Salt and pepper to taste
1/2 cup crumbled blue cheese

Mix the ground chuck, bread crumbs, salad dressing, soup mix, salt and pepper by hand in a large bowl. Shape the ground chuck mixture into four patties and arrange on a rack in a broiler pan.

Preheat the broiler on low. Broil for 6 to 8 minutes per side or to the desired degree of doneness, turning once. Sprinkle with the blue cheese and serve immediately. You may also top with crumbled crisp-cooked bacon. You may prepare up to one day in advance and store, covered, in the refrigerator. Broil just before serving.

Note: The added dressing can make these burgers too moist for the grill. For best results, use your oven broiler or a stovetop cast-iron grill pan.

Yield: 4 servings

MICHAEL'S VEAL CHOPS WITH TOMATOES AND ROSEMARY

MICHAEL KLAUBER, CO-PROPRIETOR, MICHAEL'S ON EAST

4 thick-cut veal rib chops
Salt and pepper to taste
1/4 cup (1/2 stick) unsalted butter, softened
1 pint cherry tomatoes
1/2 cup (1 stick) unsalted butter
1 (4-inch) sprig of rosemary

Preheat the oven to 400 degrees. Heat a large sauté pan over high heat until hot. Season the veal with salt and pepper and coat both sides with 1/4 cup butter. Sear the veal in the hot sauté pan for 2 to 3 minutes per side or until caramelized on both sides. Arrange the veal in a single layer in a baking pan.

Bake for 12 to 15 minutes for medium to medium-well. Remove the veal to a platter and cover to keep warm, reserving the pan drippings. Add the tomatoes, 1/2 cup butter and the rosemary to the reserved pan drippings. Season with salt and pepper. Cook until the butter is brown and the tomatoes are slightly wilted, stirring frequently. Discard the rosemary sprig. Arrange the veal on serving plates and spoon the tomato mixture evenly over the veal. Serve immediately.

Yield: 2 to 4 servings

OSSO BUCO

2 tablespoons all-purpose flour

Salt and pepper to taste

4 (10-ounce) veal shanks, 1 1/2 inches thick

1 tablespoon olive oil

1 cup minced carrots

1 cup minced celery

1 cup minced onion

1 cup dry white wine

1 large garlic clove, minced

2 (14-ounce) cans chopped plum tomatoes

1/2 cup beef broth

2 teaspoons chopped fresh rosemary

1 bay leaf

Tabasco sauce to taste

Preheat the oven to 350 degrees. Mix the flour, salt and pepper in a shallow dish. Coat the veal with the flour mixture. Heat the olive oil in a large Dutch oven over medium-high heat and add the veal. Cook until the veal is brown on all sides. Remove the veal to a platter using a slotted spoon, reserving the pan drippings. Reduce the heat to medium.

Add the carrots, celery, onion, wine and garlic to the reserved pan drippings and cook for 5 minutes, scraping the bottom of the pan with a wooden spoon to dislodge any brown bits. Return the veal to the Dutch oven along with the tomatoes, broth, rosemary, bay leaf and Tabasco sauce. Bake, covered, for 2 1/2 hours. Discard the bay leaf before serving.

Note: Serve a full-bodied, plummy, slightly spicy red, such as a Brunello or Barbaresco, to complement the stew's complexity. The other direction is a medium, dry white, such as the one used in cooking the dish—a soave made with the Trebbiano grape. Pinot grigio or sauvignon blanc would work as well. The choice here is complement versus contrast. The reds would bring spice and fruit to the table, as a counterpoint to the earthy, meaty dish. The whites would harmonize with the delicate, savory, herbal notes in the stew. The important thing is to match power with power. This is a subtle dish, so all wine pairings should be moderate, gentle vintages.

Yield: 4 servings

COUSCOUS TACOS

This meatless version of the traditional beef taco is healthy and full of flavor.

1 (14-ounce) can Mexican-style stewed tomatoes
1 cup water
1/4 cup chopped onion
5 teaspoons taco seasoning mix
2/3 cup couscous
8 ounces extra-firm tofu, drained and finely chopped
10 taco shells
1 1/2 cups shredded lettuce (optional)
2/3 cup shredded Cheddar cheese (optional)
Salsa

Combine the tomatoes, water, onion and seasoning mix in a saucepan and mix well. Bring to a boil and stir in the couscous and tofu. Remove from the heat and let stand, covered, for 5 minutes.

Spoon the couscous mixture evenly into the taco shells and sprinkle with the lettuce and cheese. Serve with salsa.

Nutrients Per Serving: Cal 148; Prot 5 g; Carbo 22 g; T Fat 4 g; Sat Fat 1 g; Chol 0 mg; Fiber 2 g; Sod 260 mg

Yield: 10 tacos

A friend who lives in the Gulf Gate neighborhood of Sarasota keeps three books on her kitchen table: a cookbook, a Bible, and a phone book. She uses the cookbook for recipes, the Bible to pray that the meal is tasty, and a phone book to make reservations if all else fails. If only she had *Simply Sarasota*!

POLENTA LASAGNA

1 (16-ounce) package frozen spinach, thawed and drained

1 (16-ounce) package refrigerated polenta

1 1/2 cups part-skim ricotta cheese

1 egg white, lightly beaten

1/2 teaspoon crushed red pepper

2 cups marinara sauce

2 ounces Parmesan cheese, grated

1/4 cup julienned fresh basil

Preheat the oven to 400 degrees. Press the excess moisture from the spinach. Cut the polenta into twelve slices and arrange the slices in a single layer in an 11×17-inch baking dish sprayed with nonstick cooking spray. Mix the spinach, ricotta cheese, egg white and red pepper in a bowl and spread over the polenta. Top with the marinara sauce.

Bake, covered with foil, for 30 minutes. Remove the cover and sprinkle with the Parmesan cheese. Bake for 5 minutes and sprinkle with the basil.

Note: Serve a light, Northern Italian red, such as a Dolcetto or a Barbera. These are light, low-tannin wines similar to beaujolais in their easy drinkability, but less "grapey" in taste than the gamay-based beaujolais (though the beaujolais would be a decent match in a pinch). It's the tomato component in the dish that drives the pairing decision.

Nutrients Per Serving: Cal 411; Prot 21 g; Carbo 61 g; T Fat 11 g; Sat Fat 5 g; Chol 28 mg; Fiber 7 g; Sod 811 mg

Yield: 6 servings

SPAGHETTI WITH ARTICHOKES

16 ounces spaghetti
1 (14-ounce) can artichoke hearts, quartered
2 to 3 tablespoons olive oil
1/4 cup (1/2 stick) butter
1 sweet onion, finely chopped
2 garlic cloves, finely chopped
Salt and pepper to taste
1/2 cup (2 ounces) grated Parmesan cheese
1/4 cup Italian-style bread crumbs

Cook the pasta until al dente using the package directions. Drain and cover to keep warm, reserving the cooking liquid. Drain the artichokes, reserving the liquid. Heat the olive oil and butter in a large sauté pan or wok until the butter melts.

Add the onion and cook over low heat until tender. Stir in the artichokes, garlic, salt and pepper. Mix in the reserved artichoke liquid and cook over low heat for 5 minutes, stirring occasionally. Stir in the cheese and bread crumbs just before serving. Toss with the pasta in a large bowl, adding as much of the reserved cooking liquid as needed for the desired moistness. Sprinkle with additional Parmesan cheese, if desired. You may add a chopped large tomato and 2 tablespoons chopped fresh parsley for color.

Yield: 4 to 6 servings

PASTA WITH GARBANZO BEANS AND ARUGULA

16 ounces pasta

1 (15-ounce) can garbanzo beans, drained and rinsed

1/2 cup (2 ounces) grated Parmesan cheese

1/2 cup olive oil

1 pint grape tomatoes, cut into halves

1 small package arugula

4 scallions, sliced

2 tablespoons balsamic vinegar

Salt and pepper to taste

Cook the pasta until al dente using the package directions. Drain and cover to keep warm. Combine the garbanzo beans, 1/2 cup cheese, the olive oil, tomatoes, arugula, scallions and vinegar in a large bowl and mix gently. Add the pasta and toss to mix. Season with salt and pepper. Serve with additional Parmesan cheese, if desired.

Yield: 4 to 6 servings

PASTA WITH TOMATOES

1 large onion, chopped
2 large garlic cloves, crushed
1/4 cup olive oil
2 tablespoons butter
12 fresh tomatoes, chopped
4 bay leaves
1/4 teaspoon oregano
1/4 teaspoon basil
Pinch of dried or fresh rosemary
Salt and pepper to taste
16 ounces flat noodles, cooked and drained

Cook the onion and garlic in the olive oil and butter in a large skillet until the onion is tender and yellow, stirring frequently. Stir in the tomatoes and cook over low heat for 30 minutes, stirring occasionally. Mix in the bay leaves, oregano, basil, rosemary, salt and pepper and cook for 15 minutes or until most of the liquid evaporates, stirring occasionally. Discard the bay leaves and spoon over the pasta on a serving platter.

Yield: 4 to 6 servings

Simply Sarasota is full of wonderful recipes from amateur cooks, as well as professional chefs. Sarasota has a high concentration of Zagat-rated restaurants for a town its size, so a great dining experience is never far away. It's no wonder that when Betsy and Doug Elder moved to Longboat Key in the 1980s, they were surprised at the first dinner party they attended: They noticed the table was not set and there were no enticing smells coming from the kitchen. After an hour, they finally asked what was for dinner. Their host replied, "This is Sarasota. We make reservations." However, with so many recipe choices throughout this book, you will be picking up the phone to invite friends over for a homemade meal.

Seared Tilapia Scaloppine with Melon Salsa, page 144

SEAFOOD

CURRIED PEANUT SHRIMP

4 (12-inch) bamboo skewers

1/3 cup pineapple preserves

1/4 cup orange juice

2 tablespoons crunchy peanut butter

1 tablespoon creamy Dijon mustard

1 1/2 teaspoons curry powder

1 teaspoon vegetable oil

1/2 teaspoon salt

1/4 teaspoon red pepper

1/4 teaspoon chili powder

1/4 garlic clove, minced

1 pound shrimp, peeled and deveined

Soak bamboo skewers in enough water to cover in a bowl for 30 minutes; drain. Combine the preserves, orange juice, peanut butter, dijonnaise, curry powder, oil, salt, red pepper, chili powder and garlic in a blender and process until smooth. Reserve 1/4 cup of the preserves mixture. Place the remaining preserves mixture in a large sealable plastic bag and add the shrimp. Seal tightly and shake to coat. Marinate for 30 minutes, turning occasionally.

Preheat the grill or broiler. Drain the shrimp, reserving the marinade. Thread the shrimp evenly on the bamboo skewers and arrange the skewers on the grill rack. Grill for 3 minutes on each side or until the shrimp turn pink, basting frequently with the reserved marinade. Spoon the 1/4 cup reserved preserves mixture over the shrimp on a serving platter.

Yield: 4 servings

LEMON SHRIMP CASSEROLE

1 pound medium shrimp
Old Bay seasoning or seasoning of choice to taste
2 cups cooked rice
1 cup (4 ounces) shredded sharp Cheddar cheese
1 (10-ounce) can cream of mushroom soup
1/4 cup (1/2 stick) butter
1/2 cup chopped green or red bell pepper
1/2 cup chopped green onions
1/2 cup chopped celery
2 lemons, thinly sliced

Bring a large saucepan of water to a boil. Add the shrimp and Old Bay seasoning and boil for 1 to 2 minutes or until the shrimp turn pink. Drain and immediately plunge the shrimp into a bowl of ice water to stop the cooking process; drain. Peel and devein the shrimp.

Preheat the oven to 375 degrees. Combine the shrimp, rice, cheese and soup in a bowl and mix well. Melt the butter in a skillet and stir in the bell pepper, green onions and celery. Sauté until the green onions are tender and stir the sautéed vegetables into the shrimp mixture.

Spoon into a 9×13-inch baking dish. Cover the top with overlapping lemon slices and bake, covered with foil, for 20 minutes. Serve immediately.

Note: For additional color, garnish with parsley. Serve with a green salad and vinaigrette.

Yield: 4 to 6 servings

HARVEST SCALLOPS AND RICE

CHEF JOSEPH ASKEW, STONEWOOD GRILL AND TAVERN

1/2 cup olive oil

2 teaspoons chopped garlic

1 1/2 tablespoons dried basil, or equivalent amount of fresh basil

1 1/2 tablespoons dried oregano, or equivalent amount of fresh oregano

3 tablespoons parsley flakes

1 teaspoon salt

1 teaspoon black pepper

2 cups vegetable juice cocktail

2 cups tomato purée

1 tablespoon sugar

1/2 teaspoon red pepper

2 pounds scallops

1 cup Italian-style bread crumbs

Hot cooked rice

Preheat the oven to 350 degrees. Heat the olive oil in a saucepan and add the garlic, basil, oregano, parsley flakes, salt and black pepper. Cook for 30 seconds, stirring constantly. Stir in the vegetable juice cocktail, tomato purée, sugar and red pepper and simmer for 30 minutes, stirring occasionally.

Coat the scallops with the bread crumbs and arrange in a single layer in a baking dish. Bake for 20 minutes. Pour the herb broth over the scallops and serve over your favorite hot cooked rice. Freeze for future use, if desired.

Yield: 4 servings

LINGUINI AND CLAMS

1/3 cup olive oil

1/4 cup (1/2 stick) butter

6 to 8 garlic cloves, chopped

4 or 5 (6-ounce) cans chopped clams

2 tablespoons (heaping) chopped fresh parsley

1 1/2 teaspoons salt

1 teaspoon pepper

16 ounces linguini

Grated Parmesan cheese (optional)

Heat the olive oil and butter in a skillet over medium to medium-high heat until the butter melts and add the garlic. Sauté for 2 minutes; do not burn. Stir in the clams, parsley, salt and pepper and bring to a boil. Reduce the heat to low.

Simmer for 30 minutes or until the clam juice has partially evaporated and the sauce has thickened, stirring occasionally. Cook the pasta until al dente using the package directions; drain. Spoon the clam sauce over the hot pasta on a serving platter and sprinkle with cheese.

Note: For a nice presentation, simply add three to five fresh, washed clams or cockles per serving during the last 15 minutes of cooking.

Yield: 6 to 8 servings

The easiest way to coordinate menu and table décor into a theme is to walk around your home picking up things from unexpected places, including the children's play room. Serving seafood? Gather up shells, coral, toy boats, maybe even a mermaid figurine to compose a centerpiece. Search far back in your china cabinet, and start looking at living room collectibles, like small books, to use as objects for table décor. Miniature pots of fresh herbs establish a casual country attitude. Is French food on the menu? Try arranging silverware in the French mode, spoons with the bowls facing down, forks with tines facing down. That's why French silverware is monogrammed on the back. And, of course, never underestimate the mood-transforming power of candles. Just make sure to use unscented candles as you don't want to take away from the enticing aromas of your thoughtfully prepared meal.

COASTAL CRAB CAKES

Creamy Dijon Sauce

3/4 cup Dijon mustard

3/4 cup sour cream

3/4 cup mayonnaise

Crab Cakes

1 egg

2 to 3 tablespoons mayonnaise

1 cup soft bread crumbs

1/4 green bell pepper, minced

1/4 onion, minced

1 tablespoon Worcestershire sauce

1 teaspoon salt

1 teaspoon black pepper

Dash of cayenne pepper

1 teaspoon dry mustard

1 pound back fin or special crab meat, flaked

1/2 cup (1 stick) butter

For the sauce, combine the Dijon mustard, sour cream and mayonnaise in a bowl and mix well. Chill, covered, until serving time.

For the crab cakes, whisk the egg in a bowl until blended and stir in the mayonnaise. Add the bread crumbs, bell pepper, onion, Worcestershire sauce, salt, black pepper, cayenne pepper and dry mustard and mix well. Fold in the crab meat, allowing the crab meat to remain in lumps.

Shape into ten to twelve cakes. Melt the butter in a skillet over medium heat and add the cakes in batches. Sauté until light brown on both sides, turning once. Serve with the sauce.

Yield: 10 to 12 crab cakes

HORSERADISH-CRUSTED SALMON

4 salmon fillets
4 teaspoons grated white horseradish, or to taste
Garlic powder to taste
Pepper to taste
1/2 cup fine bread crumbs
2 tablespoons margarine, melted

Preheat the oven to 400 degrees. Arrange the fillets in a glass baking dish and sprinkle with equal amounts of the horseradish. Sprinkle with garlic powder and pepper and any other favorite seasonings. Top with the bread crumbs and drizzle with the margarine. Bake for 15 minutes. Serve immediately.

Note: Spicy horseradish goes particularly well with gewurztraminer wines. These wines have their own spicy components. The Germans make some fine gewurztraminers, but go with the drier Alsatian style for this savory dish.

Nutrients Per Serving: Cal 291; Prot 25 g; Carbo 11 g; T Fat 16 g; Sat Fat 3 g; Chol 74 mg; Fiber 1 g; Sod 222 mg

Yield: 4 servings

From our beaches to our coral reefs, we are fortunate to have fresh fish that is caught and landed on the same day. Simply put, fresh is the only way to eat fish. Find the most reputable fishmonger you can and choose your dinner. Start with the eyes, which should be clear and shiny. The gills, behind the cheeks of the fish, should be moist and red. Scales should be tight to the skin. If you poke the skin it should spring back from the indentation of your fingers. Fresh fish looks bright, slippery, and alive, and doesn't feel sticky. And the final, most critical freshness check is the aroma. Ask the merchant to hold it up for you and take a deep whiff. It should smell like the sea, not fishy. Trust yourself on this.

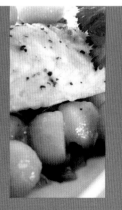

Simply Sarasota

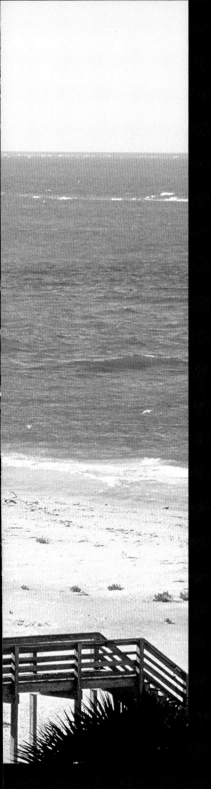

SARASOTA BEACHES

Isn't it one of life's extraordinary mysteries why food tastes so much better at the beach? Maybe it's the sky slathered with a buttery-yellow sun or speckled with glistening stars, or the appetizing salty breezes . . . or maybe the song and rhythm of the ocean waves, or the fact that no one minds if you dribbled wine on that soft, white carpet of sand. Whatever the reason, consider packing a romantic dinner for two or a family picnic lunch to enjoy at the beach. It is sure to fill your senses with the natural beauty of Sarasota's coast while tempting your palate with wonderful flavors.

FLORIDA'S FINEST GRILLED CEDAR PLANK SALMON

Don't have a supply of cedar planks in your kitchen? Not to worry . . . cedar planks are available at culinary specialty shops, or ask for them at your grocer's seafood counter.

1 (7×14-inch) untreated cedar plank

Water, apple juice or white grape juice

6 tablespoons chardonnay

1/4 cup vegetable oil

2 tablespoons soy sauce

2 tablespoons brown sugar

1 teaspoon ground ginger

Freshly ground pepper to taste

1 tablespoon vegetable oil

1 (2-pound) salmon fillet, skinned, if desired

Salt to taste

2 tablespoons butter, melted

1 teaspoon lemon juice

Immerse the plank in water in a large container. Soak for 4 to 10 hours; drain. Mix the wine, 1/4 cup oil, the soy sauce, brown sugar, ginger and pepper in a sealable plastic bag and add the fillet. Marinate at room temperature for 20 minutes, turning once. Drain, reserving the marinade.

Preheat the grill to high or to 400 to 425 degrees. Place the plank on the grill rack and grill, covered, for 3 minutes. Flip the plank with tongs and grill until light smoke develops. Brush with 1 tablespoon oil. Arrange the fillet skin side down on the plank. Sprinkle with salt and pepper and drizzle with the butter.

Reduce the heat to medium and grill, covered, for 30 to 40 minutes or until the fillet flakes easily with a fork; the time varies depending on the thickness of the fillet. Bring the reserved marinade to a boil in a saucepan and boil until reduced by half. Stir in the lemon juice and drizzle over the salmon.

Yield: 4 to 6 servings

SUN-DRIED TOMATO GRILLED CEDAR PLANK SALMON

1 (7×14-inch) untreated cedar plank
Water, apple juice or white grape juice
1/2 cup bottled sun-dried tomato vinaigrette
1/4 cup finely chopped sun-dried tomatoes
1/4 cup finely chopped fresh parsley
1 tablespoon vegetable oil
1 (2-pound) salmon fillet, skinned, if desired

Immerse the plank in water in a large container. Soak for 4 to 10 hours; drain. Mix the vinaigrette, sun-dried tomatoes and parsley in a bowl.

Preheat the grill to high or to 400 to 425 degrees. Place the plank on the grill rack and grill, covered, for 3 minutes. Flip the plank with tongs and grill until light smoke develops. Brush the plank with the oil and arrange the fillet skin side down on the plank.

Reduce the heat to medium and grill, covered, for 20 to 25 minutes. Baste the fillet with the sun-dried tomato mixture and grill for 20 to 25 minutes longer or until the salmon flakes easily with a fork. The cooking time will vary depending on the thickness of the salmon.

Yield: 4 to 6 servings

The Casey Key Fish House, south of Sarasota, is one of several local fish houses that offers outdoor dining. This *al fresco* dining appeals to a variety of patrons, including a snowy egret that lives in a nearby bird sanctuary. The egret enjoys the restaurant's fish and chips so much that when an unsuspecting tourist turns his back, the bird swoops down to steal from the plate. A word of advice: when enjoying your recipes outside, keep one eye on the food and one on the bird!

SEA BASS CORTEZ

CHEF RALPH FLORES, NORTHERN TRUST BANK

Sea Bass

4 (6-ounce) sea bass fillets

2 teaspoons Lawry's Salt-Free 17

1/2 teaspoon seasoned salt or sea salt

1/2 teaspoon lemon pepper

1 teaspoon olive oil

Lemon juice to taste

1 1/2 tablespoons white wine

2 teaspoons unsalted butter, melted

Cortez Sauce

1 tomato

1 tablespoon olive oil

1/2 red bell pepper, julienned

1/2 green bell pepper, julienned

1 small onion

1 teaspoon chopped garlic

1 bay leaf

1 1/2 teaspoons rinsed drained capers

6 kalamata olives, chopped

1/4 cup white wine

1 tablespoon chopped fresh basil

Salt and pepper to taste

1 1/2 teaspoons unsalted butter, softened

For the sea bass, preheat the oven to 350 degrees. Arrange the sea bass in a shallow dish and sprinkle with the Lawry Salt-Free 17, seasoned salt and lemon pepper. Heat the olive oil in a skillet until hot and add the sea bass. Sear on both sides and arrange in a baking pan. Drizzle with the lemon juice, wine and butter. Bake until the sea bass flakes easily with a fork.

For the sauce, make an X in the bottom of the tomato and carefully place in a saucepan of boiling water. Boil until the skin begins to separate from the pulp. Carefully remove the tomato and let stand until cool. Peel, seed and chop the tomato.

Heat the olive oil in a skillet and add the bell peppers and onion. Sauté for 1 minute and stir in the garlic. Cook for 1 minute and stir in the tomato and bay leaf. Bring to a boil and reduce the heat to low.

Simmer for 5 minutes. Mix in the capers, olives and wine and cook until the liquid is reduced by half, stirring occasionally. Stir in the basil, salt and pepper and cook for 2 minutes longer. Discard the bay leaf. Mix in the butter and drizzle over the sea bass on serving plates. Serve immediately.

Nutrients Per Serving: Cal 306; Prot 34 g; Carbo 7 g; T Fat 14 g; Sat Fat 4 g; Chol 83 mg; Fiber 1 g; Sod 445 mg

Yield: 4 servings

SEA BASS EN PAPILLOTE

1/2 cup olive oil
6 red potatoes, peeled and cut into 1/2-inch slices
6 (6-ounce) sea bass fillets or other thick whitefish fillets
9 Roma tomatoes, sliced
2 tablespoons minced garlic
3/4 cup chopped fresh basil
18 kalamata olives, sliced
Salt and pepper to taste

Preheat the oven to 425 degrees. Cut six large sheets of foil and spread on a hard work surface. Brush each sheet with 1 teaspoon of the olive oil. Layer one potato, one fillet, one and one-half tomatoes, 1 teaspoon of the garlic, 2 tablespoons of the basil and three olives in the center of each sheet of foil. Season to taste with salt and pepper and drizzle each with 1 tablespoon of the remaining olive oil. Fold the foil to enclose the ingredients and seal the edges.

Arrange the packets on a baking sheet and bake for 20 minutes. To serve, place one packet on each of six serving plates. Make an X in the top of each packet and fold back the foil; be careful of the steam. Serve immediately.

Yield: 6 servings

One local fish house patron ordered a grouper sandwich, but the waitress accidentally brought him a chicken sandwich. At the end of the meal the customer commented that his meal was delicious—but he couldn't believe how much grouper tasted like chicken.

Simply Coastal

RED SNAPPER WITH MACADAMIA CRUST

1 cup macadamia nuts
1 1/4 cups bread crumbs
2 eggs
4 (6-ounce) red snapper fillets
Salt and freshly ground white pepper to taste
1 cup all-purpose flour
2/3 cup olive oil
1 1/2 tablespoons butter
1 pound fresh spinach leaves, stems removed

Pulse the macadamia nuts in a food processor until finely ground. Add the bread crumbs and pulse until combined. Whisk the eggs in a bowl until blended. Sprinkle the fillets with salt and white pepper and coat with the flour. Dip in the egg and drain. Coat with the bread crumb mixture, pressing lightly until the mixture adheres.

Heat 1/4 cup of the olive oil and the butter in a large skillet over low heat until the butter melts. Add the fillets to the hot oil mixture and fry until golden brown on both sides. Remove the fillets to a platter and cover to keep warm.

Heat the remaining olive oil in a large saucepan and add the spinach. Cook until the spinach wilts; drain. Season to taste with salt. Spoon equal portions of the spinach onto four dinner plates and top each serving with one fillet. Serve immediately.

Note: Substitute fresh grouper or another firm, white-fleshed fish for a delicious, crispy meal.

Yield: 4 servings

142

SNAPPER ALEXANDRA

CHEF LAURENT MOUSSA

1 tablespoon butter

1 leek bulb, chopped

3 shallots, finely chopped

1 teaspoon sugar

1/2 teaspoon salt

1/4 teaspoon pepper

1 cup dry white wine

Salt and pepper to taste

1/3 cup whipping cream

2 tomatoes, chopped

1/3 cup chopped red onion

Grated zest and juice of 1/2 lemon

1 tablespoon chopped fresh cilantro

1 tablespoon olive oil

1 tablespoon butter

4 small snapper fillets

4 slices *Publix* bakery sunflower bread or
    dense country bread

1 garlic clove, grated

Melt 1 tablespoon butter in a small saucepan and stir in the leek, shallots, sugar, 1/2 teaspoon salt and 1/4 teaspoon pepper. Simmer for 10 minutes or until the leek and shallots are tender, stirring occasionally. Stir in the wine and season to taste with salt and pepper. Simmer until the mixture is reduced by half. Add the cream and cook for 7 to 8 minutes longer, stirring frequently. Mix the tomatoes, onion, lemon zest, lemon juice, cilantro and olive oil in a bowl.

Melt 1 tablespoon butter in a skillet over medium heat and add the fillets. Sauté for 8 minutes or until cooked through, turning once. Toast the bread and sprinkle with the grated garlic.

Arrange one toasted bread slice garlic side up on each of four serving plates. Top each with one fillet, one-fourth of the leek mixture and one-fourth of the tomato mixture. Garnish with sprigs of fresh herbs and serve with chilled Anjou rosé.

Yield: 4 servings

Chardonnay, with flavors ranging from crisp and lemony to full-bodied, buttery, and rich, is America's sweetheart white wine. But long before America got on the "chard" bandwagon, it was known as the dry white wine of the world. Chardonnay is the principal grape in Champagne and in white burgundies like Meursault and Puligny-Montrachet. The trick to pairing chardonnay with food is to consider the way it was made. If it was fermented and aged without wood, it will be crisp, lively, and lighter-bodied, perfect for a simple grilled fish like trout or snapper. If it was barrel fermented and aged, the chardonnay will be fuller-bodied and more appropriate for seafood and fowl served with sauces.

SEARED TILAPIA SCALOPPINE WITH MELON SALSA

EXECUTIVE CHEF PAUL MATTISON, MATTISON'S™

4 (6-ounce) tilapia fillets

Sea salt and freshly ground pepper to taste

2 tablespoons olive oil

1 tablespoon butter

2 tablespoons minced shallots

1 cup sliced very ripe honeydew melon or cantaloupe

Chopped fresh mint or cilantro to taste

Season both sides of the fillets with salt and pepper. Heat the olive oil in a large skillet and add the fillets. Sear until golden brown and turn. Continue to cook for 5 to 6 minutes longer or until the fillets flake easily. Remove the fillets to serving plates and cover to keep warm, reserving the pan drippings.

Add the butter and shallots to the reserved pan drippings and cook for 1 minute, stirring constantly. Turn off the heat and add the melon and mint, tossing to coat. Season to taste with salt and pepper and spoon the melon salsa over the fillets. Serve immediately.

Nutrients Per Serving: Cal 280; Prot 36 g; Carbo 5 g; T Fat 14 g; Sat Fat 4 g; Chol 128 mg; Fiber <1 g; Sod 77 mg

Yield: 4 servings

Photograph for this recipe appears on page 128.

TILAPIA PICCATA

1/3 cup all-purpose flour
1 teaspoon salt
1 teaspoon pepper
4 (4-ounce) tilapia fillets

1/4 cup olive oil
1/4 cup lemon juice or lime juice
1/2 cup white wine
1/2 (3-ounce) jar capers, drained and rinsed

Mix the flour, salt and pepper on a sheet of waxed paper and coat the fillets with the flour mixture. Cook the fillets in the olive oil in a large skillet until crusty and brown on both sides, turning once. Remove the fillets to a platter and cover to keep warm, reserving the pan drippings.

Stir the lemon juice into the reserved pan drippings. Add the wine and capers and mix well. Simmer over low heat just until heated through and of a sauce consistency. Return the fillets to the skillet and simmer just until the fillets have absorbed some of the sauce, turning once. Serve immediately with angel hair pasta mixed with a butter parsley sauce.

Note: The olive oil and lemon sauce with this dish would go well with an elegant, dry, oaky chardonnay. Almost all of the classic California chardonnays have that character. A more ambitious choice would be a richer white burgundy, like a Puligny-Montrachet or Meursault.

Yield: 4 servings

Sarasota is teeming with fishmongers with access to fresh fish daily. The most important thing to remember when serving seafood is to start with the freshest and highest quality fish available. Here are some simple suggestions when preparing fish:

- An old restaurant trick that ensures moist grilled fish is to rub the fish with a very thin coat of mayonnaise just before grilling. Mayonnaise is egg and oil-based, so it seals in the juices, giving your fish a moist and tender texture.

- Pan-sear salmon with the skin on over medium-high heat. Turn the salmon once and the skin will easily slide off as you remove it from the pan. Be careful not to overcook . . . the very center of the fish should be rare.

- Add crushed, shredded lemongrass to panko crumbs and pan-sear the fish in a mixture of canola oil and sesame oil for an outstanding Asian-style tempura.

BAKED TILAPIA WITH VEGETABLES

4 (6-ounce) tilapia fillets
1 tablespoon Key lime juice
1 teaspoon dried dill weed, or 2 teaspoons
  chopped fresh dill weed
1 cup coarsely chopped tomato
1/2 cup coarsely chopped red bell pepper

1/2 cup coarsely chopped yellow bell pepper
1/2 cup coarsely chopped orange bell pepper
1/4 teaspoon pepper
1/2 cup white wine
1/2 cup to 1 cup (2 to 4 ounces) shredded
  provolone cheese or Parmesan cheese

Preheat the oven to 400 degrees. Arrange the fillets in a single layer in a 9×13-inch baking dish sprayed with nonstick cooking spray. Drizzle the fillets with the lime juice and sprinkle with the dill weed. Top evenly with the tomato and bell peppers and sprinkle with the pepper.

Pour the wine around the fillets and sprinkle the cheese over the top. Bake for 30 minutes or until the fillets flake easily with a fork. Serve immediately.

Nutrients Per Serving: Cal 324; Prot 43 g; Carbo 7 g; T Fat 12 g; Sat Fat 6 g; Chol 140 mg; Fiber 1 g; Sod 301 mg

Yield: 4 servings

LEMON-STUFFED BAKED TROUT

4 whole trout, dressed
1/4 cup chopped shallots
4 lemons, thinly sliced
1/4 cup chopped fresh Italian parsley

1 tablespoon chopped fresh thyme
Salt and pepper to taste
1/4 cup (1/2 stick) butter

Preheat the oven to 400 degrees. Rub the inside cavities of the trout with the shallots and stuff with equal amounts of the lemon slices, parsley and thyme. Sprinkle the outside surface with salt and pepper.

Arrange the trout in a large buttered baking dish and top each with 1 tablespoon of the butter. Bake for 15 minutes or just until the trout flakes easily. Serve immediately.

Yield: 4 servings

Fillets de Yellowtail aux Bananas

2 (8-ounce) yellowtail fillets, skinned and boned
Salt and pepper to taste
1 cup all-purpose flour
1 ripe banana, cut into halves or quarters
1/2 cup (1 stick) butter
1/4 cup vermouth

Preheat the oven to 450 degrees. Season the fillets with salt and pepper and coat with the flour. Arrange the fillets in a buttered baking dish and top each with half the banana.

Melt the butter in a small saucepan and whisk in the vermouth. Pour over the fillets and bake for 10 to 15 minutes or until the fillets flake easily with a fork, basting frequently with the pan juices. Serve with the pan juices.

Yield: 2 servings

Sarasota local Tom Mayer grew up at his family's home and fish camp, Land's End, on the north end of Longboat Key. The property has been in his family since the early 1900s and originally belonged to his mother's great-uncle, John Savarese. Tom and his siblings were encouraged to catch and eat stone crabs, grouper, oysters, and the occasional rattlesnake. The children would fight over the grouper eye, an ingredient his father used in making a delicious fish chowder. Today, Tom still enjoys catching and smashing two clams together in order to eat them fresh, while he's swimming. Of course, you don't have to swim for your own seafood; Longboat Key offers many choices in fine dining, or choose from one of the many delicious recipes in this chapter.

Blueberry Tart, page 160

Simply
Decadent

DESSERTS

KAHLÚA CAKE

1 (2-layer) package yellow cake mix

1 cup vegetable oil

3/4 cup water

1 (6-ounce) package chocolate instant pudding mix

1/2 cup granulated sugar

1/4 cup vodka

1/4 cup Kahlúa

4 eggs

1/4 cup confectioners' sugar

1/4 cup Kahlúa

Preheat the oven to 350 degrees. Combine the cake mix, oil, water, pudding mix, granulated sugar, vodka and 1/4 cup liqueur in a mixing bowl and beat for 4 minutes, scraping the bowl occasionally. Spoon the batter into a nonstick bundt pan and bake for 45 to 50 minutes or until the cake tests done. Cool in the pan on a wire rack for 20 minutes and invert onto a cake plate. Pierce the top of the cake with a wooden pick.

Whisk the confectioners' sugar and 1/4 cup liqueur in a bowl until of a glaze consistency. Spoon the glaze over the top of the cake. Freeze for future use, if desired.

Yield: 10 servings

EAT-THE-WHOLE-THING CHOCOLATE CHIP BUNDT CAKE

1 (2-layer) package butter-recipe cake mix
1 (6-ounce) package chocolate instant pudding mix
1 cup sour cream
1/2 cup vegetable oil
1/2 cup water
4 eggs
2 cups (12 ounces) milk chocolate chips
1 cup confectioners' sugar
1/4 cup evaporated milk

Preheat the oven to 350 degrees. Combine the cake mix, pudding mix, sour cream, oil, water and eggs in a mixing bowl and beat until blended. Stir in the chocolate chips. Spoon the batter into a greased and floured bundt pan and bake for 55 to 60 minutes or until the cake tests done. Invert onto a cake plate and cool for 10 to 15 minutes. Whisk the confectioners' sugar and evaporated milk in a bowl until of a glaze consistency and drizzle over the cake.

Yield: 16 to 20 servings

Many visitors are surprised to learn that Sarasota has such active Mennonite and Amish communities, dating from the 1920s. These communities brought their customs and traditions with them, including baking scrumptious pies. Several restaurants in Sarasota offer Amish-style cooking. One offers a choice of baked, cream, or frozen pies including: Dutch apple, blueberry, cherry, egg custard, pecan, rhubarb, pumpkin, shoofly, peanut butter, banana, chocolate, coconut, key lime, chocolate peanut butter, red raspberry, and turtle pie sundae. Decisions, decisions . . .

MOLTEN CHOCOLATE CAKES

2 tablespoons butter, melted

2 tablespoons baking cocoa

3/4 cup (1 1/2 sticks) butter

12 ounces semisweet chocolate baking bars,
   broken into pieces

1/2 cup whipping cream

1 1/4 cups egg substitute (do not use eggs)

3/4 cup granulated sugar

2/3 cup all-purpose flour

Confectioners' sugar to taste

Brush twelve to sixteen muffin cups with the 2 tablespoons melted butter and sprinkle with the baking cocoa. Chill until the butter is firm. Combine 3/4 cup butter and the chocolate in a heavy saucepan and cook over low heat until blended, stirring occasionally. Whisk in the cream and remove from the heat.

Combine the egg substitute and granulated sugar in a mixing bowl and beat for 5 to 7 minutes or until slightly thickened. Add the chocolate mixture and flour and beat until blended. Fill the prepared muffin cups three-fourths full. Chill, covered, for 1 to 24 hours.

Preheat the oven to 450 degrees and bake for 8 to 10 minutes. The edges should be springy but the middle liquid; do not overbake. Dust with confectioners' sugar and serve.

Note: This can be mixed up to 24 hours in advance, then baked right before serving. Be careful not to overbake, and do not substitute semisweet chocolate chips for the baking bars!

Yield: 12 to 16 servings

CHILLED CHOCOLATE CUPCAKES

Cupcakes

1 1/2 ounces unsweetened chocolate

1/2 cup (1 stick) margarine

1 cup sugar

2/3 cup all-purpose flour

2 eggs, beaten

1 teaspoon vanilla extract

1 cup pecans, chopped

Chocolate Frosting

1 ounce unsweetened chocolate

2 tablespoons margarine

3/4 (1-pound) package confectioners' sugar

Cold brewed coffee

36 pecan halves

For the cupcakes, preheat the oven to 350 degrees. Melt the chocolate and margarine in a double boiler over simmering water, stirring occasionally. Combine the sugar, flour, eggs and vanilla in a mixing bowl and beat until blended. Stir in the pecans. Add the chocolate mixture and mix until combined. Fill paper-lined miniature muffin cups three-fourths full and bake for 12 minutes; do not overbake.

For the frosting, melt the chocolate and margarine in a double boiler over simmering water, stirring occasionally. Add the confectioners' sugar alternately with the desired amount of coffee, whisking constantly until of the desired consistency. Spread a thick layer of the frosting over the tops of the hot cupcakes and top each with a pecan half. Chill until set. Freeze for future use, if desired.

Yield: 3 dozen miniature cupcakes

APPLE DAPPLE CAKE

FARE BY THE SEA

Cake

3 cups all-purpose flour

1 teaspoon baking soda

1 teaspoon salt

2 cups sugar

1 1/3 cups vegetable oil

3 eggs

2 teaspoons vanilla extract

3 cups chopped peeled apples

1 1/2 cups pecans, chopped

Brown Sugar Topping

1 cup packed brown sugar

1/2 cup (1 stick) butter

1/4 cup milk

For the cake, preheat the oven to 350 degrees. Sift the flour, baking soda and salt together. Beat the sugar, oil, eggs and vanilla in a mixing bowl until smooth. Add the flour mixture and beat until blended. Fold in the apples and pecans. Spoon the batter into a greased 10-inch tube pan and bake for 1 1/2 hours.

For the topping, combine the brown sugar, butter and milk in a saucepan. Cook for 2 minutes or until blended and heated through, stirring occasionally. Pour the hot topping over the hot cake. Cool in the pan on a wire rack for 2 hours and remove to a cake plate.

Yield: 12 to 15 servings

HUMMINGBIRD CAKE

Cake

3 cups all-purpose flour

2 cups sugar

1 teaspoon baking soda

1 teaspoon salt

1 teaspoon ground cinnamon

1 teaspoon ground nutmeg

1 cup vegetable oil

3 eggs, beaten

1 (8-ounce) can crushed pineapple

2 cups chopped bananas

1 cup chopped pecans

1 1/2 teaspoons vanilla extract

Cream Cheese Frosting

16 ounces cream cheese, softened

1 cup (2 sticks) butter, softened

1 teaspoon vanilla extract

1 (2-pound) package confectioners' sugar

For the cake, preheat the oven to 350 degrees. Combine the flour, sugar, baking soda, salt, cinnamon and nutmeg in a bowl and mix well. Add the oil and eggs and stir just until moistened. Gently stir in the pineapple, bananas, pecans and vanilla. Spoon the batter evenly into three greased and floured 9-inch cake pans. Bake for 30 minutes or until a wooden pick inserted in the centers comes out clean. Cool in the pans for 10 minutes and remove to a wire rack to cool completely.

For the frosting, beat the cream cheese and butter in a mixing bowl until light and fluffy. Beat in the vanilla until blended. Gradually add the confectioners' sugar, beating constantly until of a spreading consistency. Spread the frosting between the layers and over the side and top of the cake.

Yield: 12 to 16 servings

KEY LIME CAKE

Key limes are a Florida specialty, and this cake is a refreshing treat. Garnish with slivers of key limes and whipped cream.

Cake

1 (2-layer) package lemon cake mix
1 (4-ounce) package lemon instant pudding mix
1 cup soda water or water
1 cup vegetable oil
4 eggs
2 tablespoons Key lime juice

Key Lime Icing

2 cups confectioners' sugar
1/3 cup Key lime juice

For the cake, preheat the oven to 350 degrees. Combine the cake mix, pudding mix, soda water, oil, eggs and lime juice in mixing bowl and beat until blended. Spoon the batter into a greased and floured 12×15-inch cake pan and bake for 45 to 60 minutes or until the cake tests done. Pierce the top of the hot cake with a wooden pick.

For the icing, mix the confectioners' sugar and lime juice in a bowl and pour over the hot cake. Let stand until set. You may freeze for future use.

Yield: 15 to 20 servings

PUMPKIN CAKE ROLL

Cake Roll

3/4 cup all-purpose flour

1 teaspoon baking powder

2 teaspoons ground cinnamon

1 teaspoon ground ginger

1/2 teaspoon salt

3 eggs

1 cup granulated sugar

2/3 cup canned pumpkin

1 teaspoon lemon juice

1 cup chopped walnuts

Confectioners' sugar for dusting

Cream Cheese Filling

6 ounces low-fat cream cheese, softened

1 cup confectioners' sugar

1/4 cup (1/2 stick) butter, softened

1/2 teaspoon vanilla extract

Confectioners' sugar for dusting

For the cake roll, preheat the oven to 375 degrees. Mix the flour, baking powder, cinnamon, ginger and salt in a bowl. Beat the eggs in a mixing bowl at high speed for 3 to 5 minutes. Add the granulated sugar, pumpkin and lemon juice and beat until blended. Beat in the flour mixture until smooth.

Spread the batter in a greased and floured 10×15-inch cake pan and sprinkle with the walnuts. Bake for 15 minutes. Invert the cake onto a clean tea towel dusted with confectioners' sugar. Roll the warm cake in the towel as for a jelly roll from the short side and place on a wire rack to cool. Unroll the cooled cake carefully and remove the towel.

For the filling, beat the cream cheese, 1 cup confectioners' sugar, the butter and vanilla in a mixing bowl until smooth. Spread the filling to within 1 inch of the edge of the cake and reroll. Arrange seam side down on a cake plate and dust with confectioners' sugar. Chill, covered, until serving time. You may freeze for future use, dusting with confectioners' sugar just before serving.

Yield: 8 to 10 servings

CREAM CHEESE POUND CAKE

8 ounces *Publix* cream cheese, softened

1 1/2 cups (3 sticks) butter, softened

3 cups sugar

6 eggs

3 cups cake flour, sifted

1 teaspoon vanilla extract

Preheat the oven to 300 degrees. Beat the cream cheese and butter in a mixing bowl until creamy. Add the sugar gradually, beating constantly until blended. Alternately add the eggs and cake flour, mixing well after each addition. Beat in the vanilla until smooth.

Spoon the batter into a greased and floured bundt pan and bake for 1 1/2 hours or until the top is light brown; a wooden pick inserted in the center will not come out clean. Remove the cake immediately to a wire rack to cool.

Yield: 12 to 16 servings

When it comes to serving dessert, do you accompany them with wine? Most people get scared away from making that final match of the meal, which can be stunning. Most dessert wines come from grapes picked very late in the harvest when at the highest level of sweetness. It is the essence of the grape. For fruit and nut desserts, stick with dessert wines from the riesling grape. Desserts that are cream-based work best with the rich intense flavor of sauternes. And what about chocolate? That is a controversial match with opinions across the culinary board. Of late, chocolate has been paired with spicy red wines, notably Spanish Rioja and Italian Sangiovese. The old standbys of port and madeira also complement chocolate. But, of course, chocolate is so dense and complete you could also pair it with a great, rich cup of coffee anytime!

ICED POUND CAKE WITH CHOCOLATE FILLING

8 ounces German's sweet chocolate

1/2 cup sugar

1/2 cup cold water

4 egg yolks, beaten

4 egg whites, stiffly beaten

Chopped nuts (optional)

1 large pound cake, sliced

8 ounces whipped cream

Combine the chocolate, sugar and water in a saucepan and cook until the mixture begins to thicken. Stir in the egg yolks and cook until thickened, stirring constantly. Remove from the heat and let stand until cool. Fold in the egg whites.

Line a large bowl with waxed paper and then line the bottom and side of the prepared bowl with slices of the pound cake. Fill the center with the chocolate mixture. Cover with the remaining pound cake slices. Chill, covered with waxed paper, for 8 to 10 hours.

Invert the bowl onto a serving plate and discard the waxed paper. Ice the side and top with the whipped cream. Serve immediately.

Note: If you are concerned about using raw eggs, use eggs pasteurized in their shells, which are sold at some specialty food stores, or use an equivalent amount of pasteurized egg substitute.

Yield: 8 servings

BLUEBERRY TART

Crust

1 cup all-purpose flour

2 tablespoons sugar

1/8 teaspoon salt

1/2 cup (1 stick) butter or margarine, slightly softened

1 tablespoon white vinegar

Tart

3 cups fresh blueberries

2/3 cup sugar

2 tablespoons all-purpose flour

1/8 teaspoon ground cinnamon

2 cups fresh blueberries

For the crust, mix the flour, sugar and salt in a bowl. Cut the butter into the flour mixture until crumbly. Drizzle with the vinegar and mix until a sticky dough forms. Press the dough 1/4 inch thick over the bottom and slightly thinner 1 inch up the side of a 9-inch springform pan.

For the tart, preheat the oven to 400 degrees. Spread 3 cups blueberries over the prepared crust. Mix the sugar, flour and cinnamon in a bowl and sprinkle over the blueberries. Arrange the pan on the lowest oven rack and bake for 40 to 50 minutes or until the crust and topping are light brown. Sprinkle with 2 cups blueberries and let stand until cool. Remove the side of the pan.

Nutrients Per Serving: Cal 293; Prot 3 g; Carbo 46 g; T Fat 12 g; Sat Fat 7 g; Chol 30 mg; Fiber 3 g; Sod 118 mg

Yield: 8 servings

Photograph for this recipe appears on page 148.

MACADAMIA, WHITE CHOCOLATE AND DARK CHOCOLATE TART

PASTRY CHEF JAMES PLOCHARSKY, MICHAEL'S ON EAST

Chef's confession: Paired with a strong cup of coffee, this combination makes an excellent early morning breakfast.

Crust
2/3 cup unsalted butter

1/4 cup sugar

Pinch of salt

1/2 egg, beaten

2 cups bread flour

Macadamia and Chocolate Filling
3/4 cup granulated sugar

3/4 cup packed brown sugar

4 eggs

1 1/2 cups corn syrup

1/4 cup (1/2 stick) butter, melted

1 teaspoon vanilla extract

1/8 teaspoon salt

1 cup (6 ounces) semisweet chocolate chips

1 cup (6 ounces) white chocolate chips

8 ounces unsalted macadamia nuts, chopped

1 ounce dark chocolate, melted

1 ounce white chocolate, melted

For the crust, combine the butter, sugar and salt in a mixing bowl and beat just until creamy. Mix in the egg until blended. Add the bread flour and beat until a smooth dough forms. Chill, covered, in the refrigerator. Roll the dough on a lightly floured surface into a round large enough to line an 11-inch tart pan with removable bottom. Press the dough over the bottom and up the side of the tart pan and freeze.

For the filling, preheat the oven to 360 degrees. Whisk the granulated sugar, brown sugar and eggs in a bowl until blended. Stir in the corn syrup. Add the butter, vanilla and salt and mix well.

Mix the semisweet chocolate chips and white chocolate chips in a bowl and sprinkle over the bottom of the frozen crust. Sprinkle with the macadamia nuts and pour the filling mixture over the top. Bake for 55 to 60 minutes or until golden brown, puffed and set in the center. Cool in the pan on a wire rack. Chill, covered, for 8 to 10 hours.

Remove the tart from the pan and place the tart on a serving platter. Drizzle the dark chocolate and white chocolate in a crisscross pattern over the top of the tart. Cut into thin wedges and serve with freshly whipped cream.

Yield: 12 to 16 servings

NECTARINE AND MASCARPONE TART IN GINGERSNAP CRUST

Tart

25 gingersnap cookies, coarsely broken
  (about 2 1/4 cups)

1/4 cup (1/2 stick) unsalted butter, melted

8 ounces mascarpone cheese

6 ounces cream cheese, softened

1/4 cup *Publix* sour cream

1/4 cup sugar

1 tablespoon grated lemon zest

1/4 teaspoon vanilla extract

1 tablespoon finely chopped crystallized ginger

Nectarine Topping

4 or 5 small nectarines, cut into halves

1/4 cup peach jam, heated

2 tablespoons finely chopped crystallized ginger

For the tart, preheat the oven to 350 degrees. Process the cookies in a food processor until finely ground. Add the butter and process until moistened. Press the crumb mixture over the bottom and up the side of a 9-inch tart pan with removable bottom. Bake for 8 minutes or until the crust darkens in color, pressing the side with the back of a spoon if the crust begins to slide. Let stand until cool.

Combine the mascarpone cheese, cream cheese, sour cream, sugar, lemon zest and vanilla in a mixing bowl and beat until creamy, scraping the bowl occasionally. Add the ginger and beat until combined. Spread over the baked layer and chill, loosely covered, for 2 to 24 hours.

For the topping, thinly slice the nectarine halves. Overlap the slices in concentric circles over the top of the filling. Brush with the jam and sprinkle with the ginger. Serve immediately or chill for up to 6 hours. You may substitute other fresh fruits such as strawberries, peaches or blueberries for the nectarines.

Note: A wine paired with an extremely sweet dessert—such as this one, made with cookies, sugar and jam—should be sweeter than the dessert. Hungarian Tokaji (pronounced "toe-kai") wines are good with sweet fruit desserts. Sauternes are also a good choice, though expensive. Madeira would also go well.

Yield: 8 to 10 servings

CUSTARD PIE

TROYER'S DUTCH HERITAGE

4 eggs
1/2 cup sugar
1/2 teaspoon salt
2 1/2 cups milk
1 teaspoon vanilla extract
1 unbaked (9-inch) deep-dish pie shell

Preheat the oven to 350 degrees. Whisk the eggs lightly in a bowl until smooth. Add the sugar and salt and whisk until blended. Heat the milk in a saucepan and skim the top to remove the scum; do not boil. Gradually add the hot milk to the egg mixture, whisking constantly until blended. Stir in the vanilla.

Pour into the pie shell and bake for 30 to 35 minutes or until the center is almost set. Remove to a wire rack to cool. Store in the refrigerator.

Yield: 6 to 8 servings

GUILTLESS FLORIDA KEY LIME PIE

1 (14-ounce) can fat-free sweetened condensed milk
1/2 cup Key lime juice
4 egg yolks
1 (9-inch) shortbread pie shell
1 cup fresh raspberries

Preheat the oven to 350 degrees. Whisk the condensed milk, lime juice and egg yolks in a bowl until blended. Pour into the pie shell and bake for 10 minutes. Cool slightly on a wire rack and chill, covered, in the refrigerator. Arrange the raspberries around the edge of the pie just before serving. Garnish with whipped cream, if desired.

Nutrients Per Serving: Cal 277; Prot 7 g; Carbo 48 g; T Fat 7 g; Sat Fat 2 g; Chol 106 mg; Fiber 1 g; Sod 57 mg

Yield: 8 servings

MARGARITA PIE

20 thin mint chocolate wafer cookies

2 tablespoons butter, melted

1 1/2 cups lightly packed white marshmallows

2/3 cup half-and-half

Juice of 2 limes (1/4 cup)

1/4 cup tequila (silver)

1 teaspoon grated lime zest

1 cup whipping cream

1 1/2 tablespoons sugar

Process the cookies in a blender or food processor until finely ground. Add the butter and process until moistened. Press the crumb mixture over the bottom and halfway up the side of a 9-inch springform pan.

Combine the marshmallows and half-and-half in a 3-quart saucepan and cook until blended, stirring frequently. Dip the saucepan in a bowl of ice water for 3 minutes or until cool. Mix in the lime juice, tequila and lime zest and stir for 8 to 10 minutes or until the mixture is cold.

Beat the whipping cream and sugar in a mixing bowl at high speed until firm peaks form. Fold the whipped cream into the marshmallow mixture and spread in the prepared crust. Freeze until firm. Cover and freeze for 2 hours to two weeks or until solid.

To serve, run a sharp knife around the edge of the pie and remove the side. Let stand for 10 minutes before serving.

Yield: 8 servings

CREAMY PEANUT BUTTER PIE

To get that "drizzled" look over the pie, put the hot fudge and peanut butter toppings into separate resealable sandwich bags. Cut a tiny end off one corner of each bag and squeeze over the pie (as if using a pastry bag). Alternate the direction of the hot fudge and the peanut butter for a true "gourmet" look to this delectable pie.

1 cup creamy peanut butter

8 ounces cream cheese, softened

1/2 cup sugar

12 ounces whipped topping

1 (9-inch) chocolate cookie pie shell

1 (11-ounce) jar hot fudge ice cream topping

2 tablespoons peanut butter

Combine 1 cup peanut butter, the cream cheese and sugar in a mixing bowl and beat until smooth. Fold in 3 cups of the whipped topping. Spoon into the pie shell, spreading to the edge to seal.

Reserve 2 tablespoons of the ice cream topping. Pour the remaining topping into a microwave-safe bowl and microwave for 1 minute or until warm. Spread the warm topping over the prepared layer and chill in the refrigerator.

To serve, spread the remaining whipped topping over the chilled layers. Drizzle with the reserved ice cream topping and 2 tablespoons peanut butter. Store in the refrigerator.

Yield: 6 to 8 servings

Simply Sarasota

HISTORIC SPANISH POINT

Ever wonder about the diet of this area's inhabitants 4,000 years ago? Scientists can answer this question because of the Indian middens found on the site of what is now Historic Spanish Point. During the 1800s, a naturalist who visited the middens referred to them as "a mighty monument erected by man to appetite." Middens are mounds that contain the debris of plants, animals, fish, and shellfish that were eaten over thousands of years. Some of the foods the ancients ate were cactus pad salad, raccoon with red wine, smoked mullet, and mullet spread. Unfortunately, or fortunately, many of those recipes were lost with the ancient inhabitants.

FARM FRESH STRAWBERRY PIE

3 ounces cream cheese, softened

1 tablespoon sugar

1 tablespoon milk

1 baked (9-inch) pie shell

1 quart fresh strawberries, hulled

1 cup sugar

2 tablespoons cornstarch

1 cup whipping cream, whipped, or
    equivalent amount of whipped topping

Beat the cream cheese, 1 tablespoon sugar and the milk in a mixing bowl until blended. Spread the cream cheese mixture over the bottom of the pie shell and top with half the strawberries.

Mash the remaining strawberries in a bowl. Strain the mashed strawberries into a saucepan, discarding the solids. Bring to a boil and gradually stir in 1 cup sugar and the cornstarch. Cook over low heat for 10 minutes or until thickened, stirring frequently. Remove from the heat and let stand until cool. Pour over the whole strawberries. Chill, covered, in the refrigerator. Spread with the whipped cream just before serving.

Note: Prepare individual graham cracker pie shells for an alternative to the large shell. Top with fresh blueberries and strawberries.

Yield: 8 servings

MOCHA TRIFLE

4 ounces German's sweet chocolate
1/2 cup strong coffee
3/4 cup (1 1/2 sticks) butter, softened
3/4 cup confectioners' sugar
6 egg yolks
2 cups heavy whipping cream, whipped
2 egg whites, stiffly beaten
18 ladyfingers, split

Heat the chocolate and coffee in a saucepan over low heat until blended, stirring frequently. Beat the butter, confectioners' sugar and egg yolks in a mixing bowl until blended. Add the chocolate mixture and beat until smooth. Fold in the whipped cream and egg whites.

Line a greased 9-inch springform pan with the ladyfingers. Spoon the chocolate mixture into the prepared pan and chill, covered, for 2 to 24 hours.

Note: If you are concerned about using raw eggs, use eggs pasteurized in their shells, which are sold at some specialty food stores, or use an equivalent amount of pasteurized egg substitute.

Yield: 8 servings

MOURÊMES AU CHOCOLAT

1 cup heavy whipping cream, chilled

1/2 cup sugar

1/4 cup water

1 cup (6 ounces) semisweet chocolate bits

2 eggs

1/2 teaspoon instant coffee granules

Pinch of salt

2 tablespoons Grand Marnier

Process the cream in a food processor fitted with a metal blade for 35 seconds. Spoon into a bowl. Bring the sugar and water to a boil in a saucepan, stirring occasionally.

Process the chocolate, eggs, coffee granules and salt in the food processor for 3 to 4 seconds. Add the sugar syrup gradually, processing constantly for 20 seconds or until smooth. Add the liqueur and process for 20 seconds. Add the whipped cream and pulse just until incorporated. Spoon into demitasse cups or a serving bowl and chill for 6 to 10 hours or until set. You may substitute a mixture of 1 teaspoon orange extract and 1 tablespoon brandy for the liqueur.

Note: If you are concerned about using raw eggs, use eggs pasteurized in their shells, which are sold at some specialty food stores, or use an equivalent amount of pasteurized egg substitute.

Yield: 8 to 10 servings

CHOCOLATE CHIP TRIFLE

2 pints whipping cream

1/4 cup confectioners' sugar

2 shots brandy (optional)

Dash of vanilla extract

1 1/2 sleeves (1-pound) package chocolate chip cookies,
   broken into bite-size pieces

10 ounces toffee bits

Chocolate syrup

Beat the cream in a mixing bowl until soft peaks form. Add the confectioners' sugar, brandy and vanilla and mix well. Reserve one-fourth of the cookies and one-fourth of the toffee bits for the topping.

Line the bottom of a trifle bowl or glass bowl with one-third of the remaining cookies. Drizzle chocolate syrup over the cookies. Spread with one-third of the whipped cream mixture and sprinkle with one-third of the remaining toffee bits. Repeat the process two more times with the remaining cookies, chocolate syrup, remaining whipped cream mixture and remaining toffee bits. Sprinkle with the reserved cookies and reserved toffee bits and chill, covered, for up to 24 hours.

Yield: 12 to 16 servings

In 1867, the John Webb family moved to a homestead in Osprey, Florida, today called Historic Spanish Point. They raised sugarcane and orange crops, and took in boarders for $10 a week. Boarders were served the fare of the day: turtle eggs, mullet, oysters, and vegetables. The Webb family built a packinghouse to protect their oranges after they lost their first crop to frost. To save money and make use of natural resources, they wrapped their oranges in Spanish moss for shipping. Unfortunately, the moss was filled with bugs and when the shipment arrived at Cedar Key, the oranges had been devoured. Luckily, none of the recipes tested in this cookbook include fruits "preserved" using this creative but fruitless technique.

SMASHING MYSTERY DESSERT

2 cups packed brown sugar

2/3 cup all-purpose flour

1 teaspoon baking soda

1 cup chopped pecans

2 eggs, lightly beaten

2 cups heavy whipping cream, chilled

2 tablespoons brandy

Preheat the oven to 350 degrees. Combine the brown sugar, flour and baking soda in a bowl and mix well. Stir in the pecans and eggs. Spread the batter in a lightly greased 9×13-inch baking dish and bake for 25 minutes or until a wooden pick inserted in the center comes out clean. Cool in the pan on a wire rack. Break the cake into bite-size pieces.

Beat the cream in a mixing bowl until soft peaks form and fold in the brandy. Fold in the cake pieces and spread the cake mixture in a 9×13-inch dish. Freeze, covered, for 4 to 10 hours or until firm. Spoon into stemmed dessert goblets and serve immediately.

Yield: 8 to 10 servings

APPLE PIZZA

1 refrigerator pie pastry

6 apples, peeled and sliced

Cinnamon and sugar to taste

3/4 cup all-purpose flour

1/2 cup sugar

1/2 cup (1 stick) butter

Preheat the oven to 400 degrees. Fit the pastry over the bottom and up the side of a pizza pan. Top with the apples and sprinkle with cinnamon and sugar.

Combine the flour and 1/2 cup sugar in a bowl and mix well. Cut the butter into the flour mixture until crumbly and sprinkle over the prepared layers. Bake for 15 to 20 minutes or until brown and bubbly.

Yield: 8 to 10 serving

BANANAS WIND SPIRIT

For a flaming finale, sprinkle this yummy dessert with rum and ignite. Once the flames diminish, spoon it into serving dishes.

2 tablespoons butter
2 tablespoons brown sugar
1 banana, quartered
1/4 cup orange juice
2 tablespoons dark rum, or 1/4 to 1/2 teaspoon rum flavoring
Vanilla ice cream

Melt the butter in a skillet over medium heat and stir in the brown sugar until blended. Reduce the heat slightly and add the banana. Cook until heated through and coated; do not overcook as the banana will become soggy and difficult to handle. Remove the banana to a platter and cover to keep warm, reserving the pan drippings.

Add the orange juice and rum to the reserved pan drippings and cook until the mixture begins to bubble, stirring constantly. Spoon the rum mixture evenly onto two dessert plates and top each plate with two banana quarters and a scoop of vanilla ice cream. Garnish with fresh mint leaves.

Yield: 2 servings

STRAWBERRY TRIFLE

1 quart fresh strawberries, sliced

1/4 cup sugar

1 (6-ounce) package vanilla instant
   pudding mix

2 cups cold milk

1 frozen pound cake

1/4 cup amaretto or orange juice

8 ounces whipped topping

1/2 cup slivered almonds

Toss the strawberries with the sugar in a colander and place the colander over a bowl to collect the juice. Let stand for 30 minutes. Prepare the pudding mix with the milk using the package directions.

Cut the cake horizontally into very thin slices. Line the bottom of a trifle bowl or punch bowl with the cake. Mix the strawberry juices and liqueur in a bowl and drizzle over the cake. Layer the strawberries, pudding and whipped topping over the cake in the order listed and sprinkle with the almonds. Chill until serving time.

Note: For a beautiful presentation, cube the pound cake and drop into individual crystal goblets. Layer the remaining ingredients in each goblet and serve.

Yield: 12 to 16 servings

CLASSIC FRUIT COBBLER

1/2 cup (1 stick) butter

1 cup all-purpose flour

1 cup sugar

2 teaspoons baking powder

1 cup milk

2 cups sliced fresh peaches, or
   1 (21-ounce) can blueberry pie filling

1/2 cup sugar

5 teaspoons ground cinnamon

Preheat the oven to 350 degrees. Melt the butter in an 8×8-inch baking pan. Mix the flour, 1 cup sugar, the baking power in a bowl. Add the milk and stir until lumpy. Pour the batter into the prepared baking pan; do not stir. Spread with the peaches; do not stir. Mix 1/2 cup sugar and the cinnamon in a bowl and sprinkle over the peaches. Bake for 45 minutes. Serve immediately or freeze for future use. You may substitute your favorite fresh fruit or pie filling for the peaches or blueberry pie filling.

Yield: 12 servings

APPLE NUT BARS

1/2 cup all-purpose flour
1 teaspoon baking powder
1/2 teaspoon salt
1 egg
3/4 cup sugar
1 cup chopped apple
1/2 cup chopped nuts
1 teaspoon almond extract

Preheat the oven to 350 degrees. Mix the flour, baking powder and salt together. Whisk the egg in a bowl until smooth. Add the sugar to the egg and whisk until blended. Mix in the flour mixture, apple, nuts and flavoring until combined.

Spoon the batter into a greased loaf pan and bake for 35 to 40 minutes or until the edges pull from the sides of the pan. Cut into bars and serve warm with ice cream or whipped cream.

Note: This recipe can be doubled and baked in a 9×13-inch dish. Cut into squares for praline-like cake bars.

Nutrients Per Serving: Cal 227; Prot 3 g; Carbo 37 g; T Fat 8 g; Sat Fat 1 g; Chol 35 mg; Fiber 2 g; Sod 287 mg

Yield: 6 bars

Mrs. Potter Palmer, a socialite and businesswoman from Chicago, moved to Historic Spanish Point in 1910. Mrs. Palmer proved to be quite progressive by installing running water and electricity, so she could live more comfortably and entertain late into the night. Her dinner parties included culinary delights such as deep fried quail, lobster stuffed with tenderloin, and fruit fondues which were served on one of twelve china patterns adorned with her favorite colors, blue and white.

FUDGY RUM RAISIN BARS

Finely ground nuts or wheat germ
3/4 cup all-purpose flour
1/2 teaspoon baking powder
1/4 teaspoon salt
1/4 teaspoon ground cinnamon
1/8 teaspoon ground nutmeg
2/3 cup packed brown sugar
3 tablespoons butter

1 egg
2 tablespoons molasses
1 tablespoon rum
1/2 teaspoon vanilla extract
1/2 cup miniature chocolate chips
1/2 cup raisins
1/4 cup confectioners' sugar
Light rum to taste

Preheat the oven to 350 degrees. Grease an 8×8-inch baking pan and sprinkle with ground nuts. Mix the flour, baking powder, salt, cinnamon and nutmeg in a bowl.

Beat the brown sugar and butter in a mixing bowl until creamy. Add the egg, molasses, 1 tablespoon rum and the vanilla and beat until blended. Stir in the flour mixture, chocolate chips and raisins.

Spoon the batter into the prepared pan and bake for 22 minutes. Drizzle the warm layer with a mixture of the confectioners' sugar and light rum. Let stand until cool; chill. Freeze for future use, if desired.

Yield: 12 bars

GOOZLY BROWNIES

2 eggs
1 cup sugar
1/2 cup all-purpose flour, sifted
2 ounces unsweetened chocolate, melted

1/3 cup butter or margarine, melted
1 teaspoon vanilla extract
1 cup coarsely chopped walnuts or pecans

Preheat the oven to 350 degrees. Whisk the eggs in a bowl until blended and mix in the sugar. Add the flour and mix well. Stir in a mixture of the chocolate and margarine. Mix in the vanilla and walnuts.

Spoon the batter into a greased 8×8-inch baking pan and bake for 20 to 25 minutes or until the edges pull from the sides of the pan; do not overbake. Cut into squares while hot and cool in the pan on a wire rack. Freeze for future use, if desired.

Yield: 16 bars

Kahlúa Brownies

Brownies

1 cup sugar

1 cup (2 sticks) butter

1 (16-ounce) can chocolate syrup

1 cup all-purpose flour

4 eggs

1 teaspoon vanilla extract

1/2 teaspoon salt

Kahlúa Cream

2 cups confectioners' sugar

1/2 cup (1 stick) butter, softened

5 tablespoons Kahlúa

Chocolate Sauce

1 cup (6 ounces) chocolate chips

1/4 cup (1/2 stick) butter

For the brownies, preheat the oven to 350 degrees. Beat the sugar and butter in a mixing bowl until creamy, scraping the bowl occasionally. Add the syrup, flour, eggs, vanilla and salt and beat until blended. Spread the batter in a greased 9×13-inch baking pan and bake for 35 minutes.

For the cream, beat the confectioners' sugar, butter and liqueur in a mixing bowl until smooth. Spread over the baked layer and chill, covered, in the refrigerator.

For the sauce, heat the chocolate chips and butter in a saucepan until blended. Spread over the prepared layers and chill, covered, until set. Cut into bars. Freeze for future use, if desired.

Yield: 2 to 3 dozen brownies

GINGERSNAPS

2 cups all-purpose flour

2 teaspoons baking soda

1 teaspoon ground ginger

1 teaspoon ground cinnamon

1/2 teaspoon ground cloves

1 cup sugar

3/4 cup (1 1/2 sticks) butter

1/4 cup molasses

1 egg

1/2 teaspoon salt

1/2 cup sugar

Sift the flour, baking soda, ginger, cinnamon and cloves into a bowl and mix well. Combine 1 cup sugar, the butter, molasses, egg and salt in a mixing bowl and beat until creamy, scraping the bowl occasionally. Add the flour mixture and beat until blended. Chill, covered, for 30 minutes.

Preheat the oven to 350 degrees. Shape the dough into 2-inch balls and coat with 1/2 cup sugar. Arrange the balls 4 inches apart on a cookie sheet and bake for 7 to 9 minutes or until crisp around the edges. Cool on the cookie sheet for 2 minutes and remove to a wire rack to cool completely. Store in an airtight container. Freeze for future use, if desired.

Yield: 4 dozen cookies

Many of the recipes in this cookbook have been handed down through generations, and are intertwined with family lore. The Gingersnaps recipe here is representative of so many recipes that are rich in family tradition and history. This recipe handed down by a much-loved great aunt, centers around the family competition for "enough" cookies. A single tin-full at holiday time, once a prize, was suddenly considered an inadequate amount. Near brawls broke out over the ownership of these tasty morsels that evoke memories of sibling rivalries, accusations over "stolen" cookies and, finally, the secret recipe revealed for all to share. So, when you sink your teeth into these chewy gems, as with many of our recipes, keep in mind that there may be a wonderful family story lurking behind. And now the recipe belongs to you, too.

CRANBERRY CREAM CHEESE COOKIES

1 1/2 cups all-purpose flour
1 teaspoon baking powder
1/4 teaspoon salt
1/2 cup (1 stick) butter, softened
4 ounces cream cheese, softened
1/2 cup sugar
1 egg
1 teaspoon vanilla extract
1 cup dried cranberries

Preheat the oven to 325 degrees. Mix the flour, baking powder and salt together. Beat the butter and cream cheese in a mixing bowl until light and fluffy. Add the sugar, egg and vanilla and beat until blended. Stir in the flour mixture and the cranberries.

Drop by teaspoonfuls onto a cookie sheet and bake for 12 to 15 minutes or until light brown. Cool on the cookie sheet for 2 minutes. Remove to a wire rack to cool completely. Store in an airtight container.

Yield: 3 dozen cookies

CHOCOLATE TOFFEE BARK

1 cup packed light brown sugar
1 cup (2 sticks) butter (do not substitute)
60 pretzel snaps or wafers
2 cups (12 ounces) semisweet chocolate chips, melted

Preheat the oven to 400 degrees. Line the bottom and sides of a cookie sheet with foil. Combine the brown sugar and butter in a saucepan and cook until the butter melts. Bring to a boil and boil for 3 minutes, stirring constantly. Pour the brown sugar mixture evenly on the prepared cookie sheet.

Arrange the pretzels randomly over the top and bake for 7 minutes. Drizzle or spread the chocolate over the hot baked layer. Chill for 30 minutes or freeze for 15 minutes. Break the toffee into pieces. You may substitute 1 1/2 cups salted peanuts for the pretzels. Store in an airtight container.

Yield: 6 servings

Contributors and Testers

The following people generously gave of their time and talent by submitting their favorite recipes or preparing recipes to test. We apologize if a name has been inadvertently omitted. Contributing chefs and restaurants are listed in the Acknowledgments.

Beverly Aach	Cheryl Burstein	Sharon Dickson-Kadel	Nancy Goldman
Joan Agnacian	Leslie Joy Busler	Emily Dorr	Marcia Goldstein
Sandra Albano	Martha Caesar	Valerie Dorr	Megan Gover
Sheila Anthony	Donna Cailor	Sandy Drettmann	Christa Guffra
Lisa Austin	Beth Cannata	Pamela Duckworth	Kari H. Hagar
Nancy Bailey	Nancy Capece-Volpe	Donna Dugan	Marcie Halibut
Shawndra Baird	Alicia Chalmers	Erin Thomas Duggan	Karen Hartman
Aly Baiter	Kay Chandler	Sharon Ehrlich	Anne E. Hayes
Amy Baker	Lydia Chapdelain	Tracy Eisnaugle	Sally Heagany
Maudie Baker-Schwartz	Jennifer Chester	Amy Elder	Ellen Hedenberg
Donna Baranowski	Teresa Christiansen	Susan Elkins	Mary Heins
Barely Blemished	Kenn Christopher	Virginia Everett	Kathleen Henderson
Committee	Georgina Clamage	Adelaide Farrell	Gervaise Henrich
Chellie Barilleau	Paula W. Clemow	Michelle Fertig	Sharon Hicks
Barbara Barrett	Rebecca Clissold	Angela Fewx	Jenny Hime
Liza Battaglia	Candice Conerly	Tish FitzGerald	Sarah Hime
Jamie Becker	Mary Conklin	Susan Foster	Bruce K. Holst
Lisa Beckstein	Claire Connor	Tanya Marks Foster	Barbara Hostetler
Patty Bettle	Mary Converse	Beth Fox	Dana Hummel
Vida Bistline	Stacey Corley	Lesley France	Lyman Hussey
Maryann Boehm	Michelle Crabtree	Michael France	Ulla Ikie
Linda Boring	B. J. Creighton	Linda Gawel	Sarah Jane Inglis
Belinda Boykin	Martha Daly	Beverley Georgi	Marianne Jackson
Veronica Brady	Margie Danahy	Kathy W. Gilkey	Rosemary Jadick
Susan Brennan	Shirley Davies	Kris Gillespie	Melba Jimenez
Marilyn Brown	Heather DeGrave	Audrey Girvan	Joyce Johnson
Jennie Buehner	Diane D'Ercole	Christine Giuffra	Kathy Jones
Marilyn Bulkley	Holly DeWitt	Dori Goldfarb	Leslie Jones
Kris Bundrant	Barbara Dickenson	Sandy Goldman	Missy Jones

Cindy Kaiser

Christie Keller

Kristi Keller

Beth Keyser

Jenny Kilcheski

Suzanne Kinder

Mary B. King

Susan Klingbeil

Susie Klingeman

Gloria Koach

Jane Koontz

Stephanie Kost

Bobbie Krohn

Kathy Krohn

Pat Kuelper

Pierina LaMantia

Linda Larkin

Nora Lavelle

Liza Leonard

Elizabeth Lewis

Kelly Liebel

Patricia Lindon

Wain Maass

Lorna Manson

Pandora Marlow-Utley

Gina Martin

Melody Martin

Mindy Mast

Cindy Masterson

Linda Maudlin

Anne McFall

Melissa McNally

Jan Shoemaker Means

Cynthia Miner

Bobbi Morgan

Susan Morrison

Mary-Lou Moulton

Diane Muhlfeld

Georgianne Davis Neal

Karin Nelson

Susan Newsome

Bill Nimz

Marjorie North

Liz Novak

Hartley O'Brien

Sally Odiorne

Brooke Oliveri

Mary Lou O'Toole

Teresa Parsons

Valerie Parsons

Debbie Partridge

Kate Pasquesi

Caryn Patterson

Henry Paul

Sarah Paul

Jessica Petro

Lisa Phifer

Dee Pinski

Anna Pohl

Kristiana Powers

Cerita Purmort

Judy Quealy

Bunny Raabe

Susan Radcliffe

Elaine Read

Kim Read

Gretchen Reimel-Moussa

Amy Remson

Dee Dee Rice

Shirley Ritchey

Robin Roach

Bitsy Robertson

Ellie Rochford

Paul Rochford

Martha Rogers

Sharon Rolle

Patty Sabers

Paulette Vitrier Schindler

Barbara Schmalzer

Holley Schroeder

Lynn Schultz

Adelaide Schuster

Carolyn Scott

Alyssa Sells

Suzie Sewall

Debbie Shapiro

Judy Shoemaker

Dawnyelle Singleton

Kim Snyder

Mary Ann Springer

Kathryn Standard

Laura Steber

Rita Steele

Julie Stewart

Sue Stolberg

Dee Stottlemyer

Angie Stringer

Jo Strobel

Barbara Stryker

Doris Stuffings

Cindy Stuhley

Amanda Stutzman

Linda Swisher

Judith Garnett Taylor

Pat J. Taylor

Mollie Thibodeau

Olivia Thomas

Dara Thompson

Tinsels and Treasures
   Committee

Minna Traugott

Mary Traurig

Chandra Tribit

Ken Tribit

Nancy Vafeas

Beth Vandroff

Varinia VanNess

Jennifer Vett

Sheryl Vieira

Lynn Wallace

Jeneen Weerasooriya

Ro Wheeler

Judith Wilcox

Lorna Wiley

Carol Williams

Nancy Windt

Donna Wingler

Lauren Wood

Heather Woolverton

Anita Worley

Jane Wright

Mark Wroblewski

Jane A. Young

Shana Zamikoff

Sarah Zanoni

Resources and Restaurants

Barbara Banks Photography, Inc.
P.O. Box 582
Sarasota, FL 34230
941-955-9077
www.barbarabanks.com

Downtown Farmers' Market
Lemon Avenue
Sarasota, FL 34236
941-951-2656
www.downtownsarasota.com
Pictured on pages 90–91

First Watch Restaurant
8383 South Tamiami Trail
Sarasota, FL 34238
941-923-6754
www.firstwatch.com

Fred's
1917 South Osprey Avenue
Sarasota, FL 34239
941-364-5811
www.epicureanlife.com

Judi Gallagher
www.judigallagher.com

Historic Spanish Point
337 North Tamiami Trail
Osprey, FL 34229
941-966-5214
www.historicspanishpoint.org
Pictured on pages 166–167

The John & Mable Ringling Museum of Art
5401 Bay Shore Road
Sarasota, FL 34243
941-359-5700
www.ringling.org
Pictured on pages 66–67

Latitude 23.5° Fine Coffee & Tea
2820 Clark Road
Sarasota, FL 34231
941-929-1616
www.latitudecoffee.com

Linens-N-Things
8372 South Tamiami Trail
Sarasota , FL 34238
941-918-9315
www.lnt.com

Marie Selby Botanical Gardens
811 South Palm Avenue
Sarasota, FL 34236
941-366-5731
www.selby.org
Pictured on pages 24–25

Mark P. Riley Luxury Real Estate Group
5581 Broadcast Court, Suite 100
Sarasota, FL 34240
941-552-5651
www.markpriley.com

Mattison's™
25 Avenue of the Flowers
Longboat Key, FL 34228
941-387-2700
www.mattisons.com

Michael's On East
1212 East Avenue South
Sarasota, FL 34239
941-366-0007
www.bestfood.com

Diane L. Muhlfeld
muhlfeld@belvoirpubs.com

Myakka River State Park
13207 State Road 72
Sarasota, FL 34241
941-361-6511
www.myakkariver.org
Pictured on pages 46–47

Kristine Nickel
kristinenickel@comcast.net
941-928-5572

Northern Trust Bank
1515 Ringling Boulevard
Sarasota, FL 34236
941-957-3660
www.northerntrust.com

Publix Super Market Charities, Inc.

Sarasota Convention & Visitor's Bureau
655 North Tamiami Trail
Sarasota, FL 34236
1-800-522-9799
www.sarasotafl.org

Sarasota Herald Tribune
1741 Main Street
Sarasota, FL 34236
941-953-7755
www.heraldtribune.com

Stonewood Grill & Tavern
5415 University Parkway
Sarasota, FL 34201
941-355-3315
www.stonewoodgrill.com

Troyer's Dutch Heritage
3713 Bahia Vista
Sarasota, FL 34232
941-955-8007
www.troyersdutchheritage.com

Van Wezel Performing Arts Hall
777 N. Tamiami Trail
Sarasota, FL 34236
1-800-826-9303
www.vanwezel.org
Pictured on page 110

Chef Jay Weinstein
jweinstein@attg.net

Nutritional Profile Guidelines

The editors have attempted to present these family recipes in a format that allows approximate nutritional values to be computed. Persons with dietary or health problems or whose diets require close monitoring should not rely solely on the nutritional information provided. They should consult their physician or a registered dietitian for specific information.

Abbreviations for Nutritional Profile

Cal — Calories	Fiber — Dietary Fiber	Sod — Sodium
Prot — Protein	T Fat — Total Fat	g — grams
Carbo — Carbohydrates	Sat Fat — Saturated Fat	mg — milligrams
	Chol — Cholesterol	

Nutritional information for these recipes is computed from information derived from many sources, including materials supplied by the United States Department of Agriculture, computer databanks, and journals in which the information is assumed to be in the public domain. However, many specialty items, new products, and processed food may not be available from these sources or may vary from the average values used in these profiles. More information on new and/or specific products may be obtained by reading the nutrient labels. Unless otherwise specified, the nutritional profile of these recipes is based on all measurements being level.

- Artificial sweeteners vary in use and strength and should be used to taste, using the recipe ingredients as a guideline. Sweeteners using aspartame (NutraSweet and Equal) should not be used as a sweetener in recipes involving prolonged heating, which reduces the sweet taste. For further information on the use of these sweeteners, refer to the package.
- Alcoholic ingredients have been analyzed for the basic information. Cooking causes the evaporation of alcohol, which decreases alcoholic and caloric content.
- Buttermilk, sour cream, and yogurt are the types available commercially.
- Canned beans and vegetables have been analyzed with the canning liquid. Draining and rinsing canned products will lower the sodium content.
- Chicken, cooked for boning and chopping, has been roasted; this cooking method yields the lowest caloric values.
- Eggs are all large. To avoid raw eggs that may carry salmonella, as in eggnog, use an equivalent amount of commercial egg substitute.
- Flour is unsifted all-purpose flour.
- Garnishes, serving suggestions, and other optional information and variations are not included in the profile.
- Margarine and butter are regular, not whipped or presoftened.
- Oil is any type of vegetable cooking oil. Shortening is hydrogenated vegetable shortening.
- Salt and other ingredients to taste as noted in the ingredients have not been included in the nutritional profile.
- If a choice of ingredients has been given, the profile reflects the first option. If a choice of amounts has been given, the profile reflects the greater amount.

Index

184

Simply Sarasota

CREATIVELY CASUAL CUISINE

Junior League of Sarasota
Attn: Cookbook
3300 South Tamiami Trail, Unit 3
Sarasota, Florida 34239
941-954-5751
jlscookbook@comcast.net
www.jlsarasota.org

Name

Street Address

City   State   Zip

Telephone   E-mail Address

YOUR ORDER	QUANTITY	TOTAL
Simply Sarasota at $24.95 per book		$
Florida residents add 7% sales tax		$
Media mail rate for postage and handling at $3.25 for first book; $2.00 for each additional book sent to same address (allow up to 2 weeks for delivery)		$
Priority mail rate for postage and handling at $5.25 for first book; $3.00 for each additional book sent to same address (allow up to 1 week for delivery)		$
Call or e-mail for gift wrapping cost		$
	TOTAL	$

Method of Payment: [ ] MasterCard   [ ] VISA   [ ] Check enclosed payable to Junior League of Sarasota

Account Number   Expiration Date

Signature

Prices subject to change without notice.

Photocopies accepted.